KU-476-131

THE
CONSULTANT

THE
CONSULTANT

IM SEONG-SUN

Translated by An Seon Jae

R A V E N 🐦 B O O K S
LONDON • OXFORD • NEW YORK • NEW DELHI • SYDNEY

RAVEN BOOKS
Bloomsbury Publishing Plc
50 Bedford Square, London, WC1B 3DP, UK
29 Earlsfort Terrace, Dublin 2, Ireland

BLOOMSBURY, RAVEN BOOKS and the Raven Books logo
are trademarks of Bloomsbury Publishing Plc

Originally published in Korean by EunHaeng NaMu Publishing Co., Ltd.
First published in Great Britain 2023

Copyright © Im Seong-sun, 2010
English-language translation © An Seon Jae, 2023

Im Seong-sun has asserted his right under the Copyright,
Designs and Patents Act, 1988, to be identified as Author of this work

This book is published with the support of the Literature Translation Institute
of Korea (LTI Korea)

This is a work of fiction. Names and characters are the product
of the author's imagination and any resemblance to actual persons,
living or dead, is entirely coincidental

All rights reserved. No part of this publication may be reproduced or
transmitted in any form or by any means, electronic or mechanical, including
photocopying, recording, or any information storage or retrieval system,
without prior permission in writing from the publishers

No responsibility for loss caused to any individual or organization acting
on or refraining from action as a result of the material in this publication
can be accepted by Bloomsbury or the author

A catalogue record for this book is available from the British Library

ISBN: HB: 978-1-5266-5414-4; TPB: 978-1-5266-5415-1;
EBOOK: 978-1-5266-5413-7; EPDF: 978-1-5266-5411-3

2 4 6 8 10 9 7 5 3 1

Typeset by Integra Software Services Pvt. Ltd.
Printed and bound in Great Britain by CPI Group (UK) Ltd, Croydon CR0 4YY

To find out more about our authors and books visit www.bloomsbury.com
and sign up for our newsletters

CONTENTS

The Consultant

Trotsky, having lost the power struggle against Stalin, fled to Mexico. Some historians say that if he had stayed in power as a moderate rationalist, the future of the Soviet Union and of Communism might have been very different. But he was neither cowardly nor cold-blooded enough compared to his rivals. Life is such that a person's positive qualities can bring him down at a critical moment.

None of Trotsky's family members escaped Stalin's watch. Pursued endlessly, they were purged one by one. It wasn't just the family. Neither his political colleagues nor his friends survived. Trotsky, who defected, was virtually confined to a small room alone. Half the world was after him. But Stalin was not satisfied with that.

One day Trotsky's secretary fell in love with a man, a man of rare character, polite and serious. The secretary introduced Trotsky to this kind, good man whom she loved. The two made common cause and became close friends, since the lonely older man was so hungry for human kindness. The younger man was not in a hurry: he waited until he had the trust of Trotsky and those who were guarding him. Mistakes were not tolerated where he came from.

One afternoon, a year later, the two were talking alone. There were no guards, no followers with them. The man did not hesitate but drove an ice axe into the top of Trotsky's head. It took many years for him to be identified, but people already knew who had ordered the act. The acronym NKVD, the bureau to which the man belonged, stands for the 'People's Commissariat for Internal Affairs', and was renamed the KGB after World War II, while he was still in prison. The real irony is that the founder of the NKVD was none other than Trotsky himself. It had been created after the Russian Revolution as a police organisation to resolve the absence of security in the Soviet Union.

Some people call this a murder. But it was in fact a declaration that no one could stand up to Stalin.

Suppose we take the most successful murder as an example, such as that of Kurt Cobain, the lead singer of the rock band Nirvana. There is a conspiracy theory suggesting that he was murdered. The list of suspects includes his beloved wife, a superfan, a management company, members of the same band, rival bands and even the CIA. As with most conspiracy theories, the logic is weak and it's nothing but exaggeration.

If you're a fan of Kurt Cobain, it offers a few hours' worth of fun, and it's quite exciting. However, if an investigation is carried out thoroughly, it can also be refuted in a few hours. No one is going to believe in the murder theory unless it's someone with very odd tastes because his suicide note is so wonderful, just like him, and his life and songs play perfectly with suicide as a full stop. With his death, his records sold like crazy, his last moments became a myth and the place of his death became a shrine. Some make money, some are sad, some have regrets, but no one is unhappy with it. That's exactly what a truly great murder is, a murder with satisfaction all round. People don't believe he was murdered. Even I don't know if he was really murdered. If it was a murder, I'd want to say it was a really great one. So that's one example.

It is really difficult to cite an example of a great murder.

First, their frequency is very rare, as shown by the word 'great'. Only murderers will know how many murders can rise to the realm of greatness. That goes hand in hand with the second reason. A truly great murder is not recognised as a murder. Obviously, if anyone who kills or orders a killing or commits one is acting with the intention of showing off, like Stalin, that is not a murder, it is terrorism. There are people who mistake the two for the same thing. A really good murder, as Kurt's example suggests, is driven by violence, but is done without asserting itself.

For this reason, it is almost impossible to recognise a great murder. The moment someone realises it's a murder and proves it, the murder degenerates into something petty and normal. Therefore, the greatest murders are by no means ambiguous regarding the cause of death. Everyone acknowledges the cause of death, believing that they know what it is.

This is a story about the Company I go to work for. No, it's not appropriate to say 'go to work' because I don't actually go to work. So, to be more exact, it's the Company I work for. Maybe you work for the same Company. Even then, we wouldn't know each other. Because the Company is like that. Maybe you work for the Company and don't even know that you're doing so. You yourself may not even know that you belong to the Company. A former employee of a large company I met in the DRC told me: 'These days, people don't even know where they're working and who they're working for.'

Indeed, people do not know where they work and who they work for. Most of the people I met were like that. Of course, I'm not so different either.

Restructuring

After Manager Lee's early retirement due to restructuring, in the wake of a series of misfortunes such as bills in arrears, several things happened that were impossible to write off as mere bad luck. Just as he retired, his wife met another man and ran away, using their house as collateral for a loan – but that was only a prelude to the disasters that were to come. After he was swindled out of the house – which he had expected to provide him with a lump sum for his retirement, prepared as severance pay – he found himself living on the street within a matter of days. The last straw was an assault case involving his beloved only son. The victim's family demanded a ridiculously high settlement, and there was nothing to be done about it. Lee, who was generally noted for his gentle and serious personality, went to the police station and caused a disturbance. He protested loudly at the police's intention of arresting his son, who had made a mistake in a minor dispute, while they had not even looked for his wife after she ran away. All he got in exchange was a night on the cold floor of a detention cell.

Two days after leaving the police station with a glum look on his face, he was found dead in his garage, which was due to be auctioned off separately from the house. Lee was lying in a comfortable position in the driver's seat of his car, with the back reclined. At his feet was a large bottle of the soju used to make fruit liquor, and the garage door was closed. His blood alcohol levels showed he was intoxicated, as expected, and the cause of death was carbon monoxide poisoning.

According to Kim, a real estate agent who was the principal witness, the car's exhaust gas was almost undetectable even when the garage door was first opened. The garage was completely sealed in winter, so it wouldn't have taken long for the car to become a small gas chamber. The police concluded the case hurriedly. It was not clear whether it was a suicide or an accident, because no suicide note was found. The bereaved family claimed that Lee would not have committed suicide because he was a Catholic, but that he was drunk and had fallen asleep. Was his death just bad luck?

If it was not bad luck, someone must have been responsible. Was it the company that left him unemployed in his prime, the wife who ran away, the real estate agent who cheated on his taxes, the son who used his fists recklessly or the son's victim who would not settle? Perhaps it was because of the police, who blindly detained him overnight without listening to his desperate circumstances? Any of them might have been able to prevent this chain of misfortunes. But no one did. The police only acted according to the law, and the son's victim acted as reasonably as possible to gain compensation for damages suffered. His son only expressed his sudden despair at his family's misfortune in the form of violence, and his wife made a decision to pursue her own happiness when the shadow of unemployment fell over a marriage that had been less than happy for the past eighteen years. The same was true of the company. The company, wanting to minimise costs and maximise profits, judged that he was unfit to work. Their actions were therefore reasonable in light of their desires. Everyone deserves to be a follower of Adam Smith, made a little grumpy by invisible hands. Lee's misfortune seemed to be no more, no less than it really was. Such was the fate of those who were not suitable for the company. Even those who give strength to what is known as the neck of the middle class must face the vastness of the world when the title written on their business cards disappears. Anyone can go tumbling down a slope in a flash.

I also have a business card. It's pretty cool, but unfortunately, it's rarely used. So I want to take this opportunity to show it off. The background is white, a little greenish, but such a faint green that you can't tell unless you look closely. It is not clear whether it was intended or not, but the card has a rough, irregular texture, an irregular or a faint pattern, but that is just a visual sensation. Actually it's soft to the touch, very smooth. And it hardly ever gets wrinkled. The lettering is all in English Gothic, with slightly rounded ends, but is firm-looking. The company's name and my title are printed simply in the corner, and my name is in the centre. Flip it over, my phone number and email address at the bottom are as simple, neat and beautiful as can be. My Manager, who designed this business card, boasted that the material was mixed with cotton.

'It's like paper, but it's real cotton. It's similar to the ingredients in US dollar bills. I don't think you can find it anywhere else.'

I think she deserves to be proud. Really. I'm just sorry I don't use them often. I usually work alone at home and send off the results in a postbox. On the day I received my business cards from my Manager, it had been almost three months since we'd first met.

'You probably won't have much use for them. But you know. The Company knows that you'll need them at some point, so …'

She shrugged her shoulders with a look of regret. I could understand. It was too beautiful a business card to keep in your wallet. If Andy Warhol had seen this business card, he might have copied some, painted them in different colours, framed them and hung them on a wall. But it was at a high-school alumni reunion a few years later that I finally used them.

There had been several incidents that year, so it was an exceptionally difficult time. I wanted to believe that I was living a normal life, so I needed a very normal and casual group of people to be around. If it weren't for that reunion, I might have gone to a church, a chapel, a temple, even a mosque. Of course, it is undesirable to have a religion for work. No, really, I was afraid they might see it like that. But now that I think about it, the Company wouldn't care if I had a religion, as long as it didn't interfere with my job. The Company is always generous in that respect. But at the time, there was no room for such thoughts. That is because it was a time when I was being very cautious in conjunction with various events. So I was excited when I heard about the reunion, and to exaggerate a little, I felt saved. In the end, I even wore a new suit. If anyone knew I was excited, they would have thought I was meeting my first love at the reunion. But I had graduated from a typical boys' high school, and I'm not gay. I know, that's the kind of thing that people love to hear about. So I'm sorry. But it's all about the

Company and I'm a very normal person except for my job. And I don't think even my job is that special, after going to the DRC.

As soon as I entered the room where the reunion was being held, where people in suits were standing around, I realised two things. That I looked like a normal person when I was among them, and that I didn't have many friends in high school.

In my school days, I had gone unnoticed. There must have been at least one such student in any class, people who have an exceptionally weak presence, who only exist as part of the background, like desks and chairs, when people remember the class. I wasn't a particularly gloomy student, nor was I bad at relationships or bullied, I was just non-existent. Even the type of friends who bullied the weak to show off that they were tough never touched me because I didn't come into their cognitive domain. Mine was the name that the teacher never called out when he randomly called out a name in class and made them read. Because of this, all the alumni who met me were nervous. Shaking hands while their faces showed they were furiously trying to recall who I was, I'll admit, was a bit of a treat. I'm a normal and courteous person, so I didn't bother them by not remembering their names. Many of them even remembered me when I said my name. However, it was similar to being able to remember whether the class motto was located on the right or left side of the national flag. That's what it's like to leave no memories. So everyone felt sorry for me.

The majority of responses were similar. First, people were embarrassed, then recalled memories, pretending to be as glad as they could, exchanging business cards, leaving a few brief compliments and then disappearing, shouting the name of someone else behind my back in an overly loud voice. A few were different. Maybe they had experienced the same thing that had happened to me and knew what it was like. They tried to hold a conversation, even formally; they were almost desperately looking for something to talk about. But I felt sorry for them because I was enjoying myself in my own way.

One of those figures, who had been the class president when I was in third grade, looked at my business card, which read 'Consultant', and asked, 'By the way, what are you consulting about, exactly?'

'Nothing special, restructuring.'

The class president's expression changed at that. I could feel a change in the eyes of others as they very slowly turned to look at me, like drops of ink spreading out in clear water. I could hear voices whispering behind my back. I couldn't help it. Restructuring always stimulates our generation's survival instinct.

Later that night, one guy grabbed me by the collar on the way from one bar to another. He was famous for fighting quite a bit when we were in school. He suddenly punched me. I almost fell to the ground. My cut lip tasted like iron. When I looked up, he was being restrained by other friends. After swearing at me, he suddenly burst into tears like a child. The friends released their grip, and someone comforted him. I stood blankly with a puzzled look on my face.

The class president approached me and said, 'Try to understand. It seems he's working for a water purifier company now after restructuring by his bank a few days ago.'

I could guess what he had to go through to sell water purifiers. He needed someone to blame. When men gather together, they tend to develop a fever, and he was at the bottom of the pyramid called 'Alumni'. That day must have been an intolerable insult for him, who had always been at the top of the food chain in his memories. After all, this was the world of men. This was a normal reunion, and I was relieved. I was a little less relieved because I'd been hit and I'm not the kind of person who deserves a beating. Having proved mediocre, there was no reason to follow my classmates anymore. I came back home, checked my cut lip and drank alone. My favourite animal series was on the documentary channel. It was about how mountain gorillas gather, establish rank and mate. A group of apes hovered around me in the dark room.

Since then, I can count on one hand the number of times I have used my business cards. There are still two boxes in a drawer at home that have not been opened. My Manager doesn't ask me if I need more because she knows my situation well. That's how she handles everything. I'm so adept at doing everything on my own. If I liked my job, she'd be the biggest reason. The problem is that I don't like my job very much. I want to ask you, do you like your job? I hope you don't forget until this is over that I'm no different from anyone else.

As shown on my business card, I am officially a consultant working for a company and I consult on restructuring. As the word 'consult' suggests, I do not roll up my sleeves myself. I just tell people how to deal with things. When an establishment has a person causing serious damage or trouble, the organisation, or sometimes an individual, contacts the Company. Then the Company consults me and I make a plan. Based on the plan, the Company seeks experts and restructures neatly. The restructuring is done so neatly that the targets for restructuring never ask for severance pay on leaving. Of course I get the money instead. But it doesn't cost the Company or whoever hired the Company a single penny. The money is usually given in white envelopes and the envelopes say 'Condolences'. Of course someone might cry, someone might send a wreath, someone might play cards during the wake. In any case, the restructuring will be completed after the funeral, whether it is burial or cremation.

Lee's death was treated as an accidental death. Thanks to the life insurance he had signed up for as a new employee, his son was able to reach an agreement with the man he hit. Exactly three months later, Lee's wife knelt down in front of his grave and shed tears of repentance. Her recent fling, which was impetuous and intensely passionate, had ended with remorse. The man who had approached her was from the Company. The Company had swindled Lee out of his house, and the victim who was beaten up after arguing with his son was also a man hired by the Company. The police who put him in a cell for obstruction of justice may also have been under the influence of the Company.

When Lee retired, he carried off something dishonourable that he ought not to have carried off. Manager Lee's firm consulted the Company about this problem and the Company consulted me. That's why I planned a series of little misfortunes for him. He didn't accidentally fall asleep in the car; he didn't accidentally get drunk. He was not the last person to start his car. That's not actually what happened to Manager Lee.

I hope you don't misunderstand. I haven't hurt or harassed anyone, let alone killed them. The violence I practise is to some extent always on a textual level. You may wonder if it's possible to be a killer who doesn't kill people, but as far as I know, I've been indirectly involved in at least fifty natural deaths. Yes, the key word is natural death. In movies, novels and cartoons, killers wear flashy suits and carry flashy weapons, causing flashy incidents and killing people noisily. Of course, that's because it's fun and thrilling. But in reality you rarely want to present your opponent with such a death. You might need a hitman like that if you're a godfather in the Mafia and you're at war with the opposition. They need to show off their power. But even mafias kill their targets secretly, if possible, and send fish wrapped in newspaper to their rival organisation. Then they suggest that someone from that other organisation is stuck under Brooklyn Bridge or buried in a cement floor beneath a newly built housing complex. They are also business people, and in business it's good to have no trouble. So if you're a son with a delayed inheritance, a head of a troubled union or a politician who has to face a candidate who's almost certain to win an election, your opponent's unnatural death is not a good solution. This is because, at least in countries where there is a legal system, the following or nearly identical article exists in criminal law:

Article 31 (Abetting) (1) A person who commits a crime by abetting another person shall be punished with the same sentence as the person who commits the crime.

So, few people love a noisy death. The same is true from a killer's point of view, too.

In movies and dramas, we often see people threatening, 'You could die without anyone knowing, not even a rat or a bird.' There is something that they overlook. Even if someone is killed without a sound, it is still difficult to dispose of the body. That is the reason why undertakers make a lot of money, because the job requires skill, it's messy and it's hard work. When a person dies, he or she simply becomes a lump of trash weighing just as much as when alive. As it rots, it smells bad, and if someone sees it, it becomes troublesome. Furthermore, it is almost impossible to transport alone. That's why many murderers, including serial killers, cut up bodies into pieces. Many murderers have agonised over this problem, from those who grind up the bodies and dump them down drains, to those who dissolve them in sulphuric acid or cut them into pieces and feed them to dogs and cats. In most cases, they are arrested because of the problem of how to deal with the body. At this point, you can understand why so many serial killers simply abandon the bodies, the decisive evidence of their crimes. After all, the best way to dispose of a body is to leave it to the bereaved family. Whether they bury it or burn it, they deal with it as they please. But if the dead person has died in an unnatural way, the body is the clearest sign of a crime, and in principle our justice system is tough on crime. In short, if someone kills somebody and dumps the body, the police will chase after them like crazy. So a natural death is needed. Then it is easy to dispose of the body and there is no problem. Crime demands a 'prerequisite'. This term, 'prerequisite', which relates to plausibility, put in easy terms, applies to our work.

If anyone wants to kill someone, they should kill as naturally as possible. If no one recognises it as illegal, the law will condone it.

In that instance, therefore, the death is natural for murderers, for hard-working policemen and for the sake of the law. Like in the famous crime movie *Chinatown*, if you have plenty of money or enough power, you can kill someone and get away with it. However, if you want to get away with what happens after killing someone, still you will suffer irreparable damage to either your power, your honour or your wealth. Ultimately, there is a harsher and longer period of hardship awaiting you than the time taken to commit the murder itself.

That's why people like myself are needed. If you put a lot of knowledge and a lot of manpower into planning carefully, surpassing law enforcement agencies and basing yourself on the rich experience of professional people, it is by no means impossible to execute a natural death that no one can recognise as a murder. As in the case of Lee. Everyone agrees that it was a death worth accepting, and they sincerely mourn his misfortune. Then they go home, kiss their sleeping children on the forehead and feel grateful that they didn't experience a similar misfortune. I understand that you want to blame me. But I'm no different from an accountant, a lawyer or a fund manager. Even death is just a service product. How much more humane than being dumped in a cement-filled drum in the sea and so got rid of. I make death something tragic and realistic and satisfying at the same time. This is my expertise. You can call me a killer if you want. But I call this job restructuring. There are many kinds of restructuring in the world, but death is the one real restructuring. A common misconception is that people believe restructuring is done in order to create a better and more reasonable new structure. As an expert, the reality is this: a real structure never changes, it's always only the members of the structure that disappear.

The Company

The company name on my business card is not at all the name of the Company I'm talking about. It's kind of a paper company. Of course, when I say paper company, I don't mean it's just a phantom company merely registered on paper. If you see my business card then search for the company's name on the internet, you can find it easily. There is a homepage, contact information is available, even offices and staff exist. Of course, it's labelled as a minor Seoul branch. I'm paying taxes and four major kinds of insurance through this company. If I get a stomach ulcer from the stress of planning murders, I can benefit from the company's medical insurance. It's a really good job considering the price of local health insurance. And although it won't happen, even if the police should catch me, at least they won't be able to charge me with tax evasion like the Mafia. I'm paying everything from income tax to the National Pension Scheme. I can even receive unemployment benefits if I get fired from the camouflaged company.

I'm not the only one. It's the case with all the staff in the office. And the staff at this branch are actually doing something. They work on things like documents, requests and data research emanating from the headquarters. Of course, there is no headquarters. Most of the work directed by the headquarters involves researching necessary professional references and information related to what I do. The employees believe they are working for a small foreign research company. The point is this: this camouflaged company exists purely for me.

I don't mean to brag about myself. I'm simply trying to explain the way the Company works. The Company has me locked up in a small enclosed space that starts with me and ends with me. If someone pries, the ghost company on my business card will emerge, and no matter how hard they search, they'll go spinning around inside it, like a Möbius strip.

All the instructions from the real Company are delivered to me through my beautiful Manager. All I know about the Company is my Manager's phone number and the postbox that I send the results to after the work is done. A postbox might sound funny. I know. Isn't this the world of the internet? But the internet leaves a trail. Of course, I suppose I could try to cover my tracks but it's a very cumbersome, incredibly troublesome process, it takes a lot of equipment and it has to be done well. Therefore, the Company uses traditional methods. Camouflaged CIA companies are also said to still use postboxes. I don't know about our Korean National Intelligence Service. At any rate, a postbox is an established method of communication used by various intelligence agencies.

The Manager provides all the conveniences I need to do my job. Of course I want to have personal and physical contact with her, beautiful as she is. And that's the convenience I'd most like to be offered. She always says it's impossible under company regulations. I don't know if that's true. But there's no way to find out if she's using the Company's name to deceive me. That is a matter of great regret because she is incredibly sexy. I can't forget the first day I saw her. Maybe I'll never forget it. Because it was the day I decided to accept this job.

I was sitting in the cafe where we'd agreed to meet, but I couldn't make up my mind. It was just before the appointed time. My coffee cup was already bottoming out, and the clock was heading for three. The test was over, and I had been told that the result was a passing grade, but I felt uncomfortable. My bank had already received the equivalent of several years' salary of my peers, and the shock I'd felt at first had by now disappeared and turned into something I could handle. But deciding whether to become a killer wasn't a simple task. The Company wasn't a group of justice killers or judges – who didn't have to have a guilty conscience, as in comic books and movies – not that I believed that, either. There was no grand ideology, religion or philosophy, it was just about killing people for money. It was a problem unlike any of the biggest decisions I'd made so far in life, whether to 'join the army because of my grades' or not. There might not be many, but it was clear that innocent people would be among the targets to be killed. I wasn't sure I could handle their deaths. I thought it must be harder than I imagined, no matter what I imagined. Or rather, to be more honest, I was worried about the pain I would feel when I killed them off, rather than the people I would kill themselves. At that time, I was younger and tended to overestimate my morality and conscience.

The global relief of caffeine from worldwide franchise beans was of no use to me. Outside the window was a bright, sunny afternoon, and everyone passing by looked happy. The cafe was no different. As people queued before the menu marked 'Fair Trade', their only worries were probably about what kind of coffee to drink.

When I saw them, I naturally sighed. Like them, I ought to get a normal job. On the one hand, there was regret. It wasn't too late to get a normal job. Although my grades were poor, I had not graduated from school yet, and I could think of it as a year spent preparing for a job that I had neglected by about half a year more than others. But frankly, they must have less money in the bank than I did. And that gap was only going to widen. The aftermath of the 1997 IMF crisis was still being felt in the outside world, and it was not easy to get a job. Also, I wasn't sure if the Company would let me go, because by this point I already knew too much. Above all, the most confusing part was the fact that I had done a lot better than I expected. To borrow the expression of the ethics textbooks from my school years, the Company would be a perfect place for my self-realisation.

Just then, a man who was smoking came into view outside the window, and a thought crossed my mind.

No matter how many people I kill during my lifetime, it'll still be fewer than the man who created the adverts for the cigarette he's smoking.

Cigarettes kill millions of people but no one is blaming the people who promote them. In the past, the Korea Tobacco and Ginseng Corporation was one of the best employers for graduates. Death is also being sold by the state. Do they feel guilty? How many people might I manage to kill? A hundred? Two hundred? It was clear that it would be fewer than the deaths spewed out by tar and nicotine.

I lowered my head. The clock was marking three o'clock. I thought of my bank balance. I swallowed hard and dialled the number. After just three ringing tones, someone answered the phone. There was a heavy silence. I took a deep breath.

'I'll do it.'

The phone was cut off at that moment. Hearing the call end, I looked at my phone blankly. Just as I was about to press the button to call again, someone sat down in the empty seat opposite me.

'Hello. I'll be in charge of you from now on.'

A delicate white hand appeared over the table. The fingers were so thin they seemed likely to break, and blue veins emerged along the wrist. I looked up and stopped breathing. Just then, if someone had asked me whether I believed in the existence of the succubus, I would have said yes. She was like a creature created from my stolen dreams, my wet dreams. She wore a sensual red dress, red high heels and mesh stockings, her hair was cut short. Because of that, her small head looked even smaller, and her well-proportioned figure was not only more striking, but also gained a strange, neutral charm. I had to say something but I couldn't think of anything. Everything turned red and white at the same time. Then she smiled, slightly derisively, as if she knew what I was thinking. A sigh emerged from my lips like a balloon deflating. At that she snorted scornfully, as if telling me to listen to her, and withdrew the hand she had held out for me to shake. I lowered my head. I could feel my ears reddening.

'You're cuter than I expected.'

There was a moment of silence. She crossed her legs. As her legs overlapped, her white thighs could be glimpsed beneath the short miniskirt. I couldn't take my eyes off them. I swallowed again. Then suddenly I realised what I was blankly staring at and looked up, startled. She gazed out of the window, turning her head as if it didn't matter.

I carefully studied her face. Her appearance was close to my dream ideal, but there was something artificial about it. Her nose seemed to have been lifted a bit and an edge seemed to have been shaved off her chin. Even though I couldn't be sure, her large eyes with their Western feel must also have been the result of enlargement and double eyelid surgery.

A cold chill ran up my back. Her face was the workmanship of the Company. I couldn't understand how it was possible. My taste in women, especially when masturbating, is something I had never told anyone about, let alone the Company. But more chilling than that, it was only three minutes ago that I had decided to say yes to the job. It was clear that it would have taken at least half a year for any facial swelling to subside after surgery. If you don't know much about the Company, you might think of my Manager's appearance as a subtle coincidence. But looking back on everything I'd been through prior to sitting in this cafe, there was no chance that her fixed face would fit my sexual fantasies simply by accident. At least half a year prior to joining the Company, they already knew the specific forms of my desires and the decisions I would make. My face stiffened without my realising it.

'You don't look stupid. That's a relief. If the person who's working with me is stupid, it's me who'll have a hard time.'

At that, my erection weakened because I realised that even my feelings were now those intended by the Company. The Company literally created such managers to make people stand in fear and awe of them, and to ensure maximum efficiency and convenience in working. For heaven's sake, how much did the Company know about me? I had believed that I was choosing, but that was just my illusion.

That's how the Company works all the time. It seems like they're giving you the right to decide, but in fact you have no choice. The Company knows everything, or at least as much as they need to know, and is involved in everything. And it's not work that dominates desires. Even I know that. It's things like water, air, money. If you're not afraid of the Company, you don't know the Company yet. I sometimes have nightmares about them. In my dreams, I make a mistake and it's me who's being pursued by them. And there is no avoiding them. You won't understand this fear yet, but that's because you have no idea of the Company. And that's the scariest thing about them.

Choice

It was shortly after I was discharged from the military that the Company revealed its existence in my life. Before joining the army, I had been crazy about an online mystery story club, leaving only my name on the school attendance register while I played truant. I logged in and out of the bulletin board dozens of times a day and published a series of stories. It was the age of online fiction, before the World Wide Web had been widely heard of. Every day, books came pouring out with a new ID on the cover, and rumours circulated on the bulletin board that anyone with a high number of views could go looking for a publisher.

I also had the same dream at the time. I used to vaguely imagine that as a popular online writer I could publish books offline, in the real world. In fact, at least in our club, it was quite a frenzy. Everyone wanted to sit next to me at the offline parties, and some people used to buy me drinks and gifts, telling me confidentially that they were enjoying reading my work.

The problem was that mystery novels were a very minor genre, even though they were popular literature. No matter how many people were killed, or how peculiarly, or what genius caught the criminal by deduction, they could not keep people's interest next to stories of fantasy and martial arts. There was no way they could outdo a knife flying through the air under the control of a ghost, a wizard dropping meteorites or a dragon spitting fire.

One literary club had tens of thousands of daily visitors and worked with more than a thousand views, but in our club, there were hundreds of daily visitors at the most, and the most read posts never exceeded one hundred views. According to the system operator, who I was close to at the time, the management staff called that figure 'The Wall of One Hundred'. Nowadays, quite a lot of mystery novels have been published, but back then, there were no proper mystery novels apart from the Agatha Christie series produced by one publishing company. And those were shelved with the children's books.

Eventually, my dream remained a dream, and I received my call-up papers along with a second-year report card with the same grade as the Chunichi Dragons' Sun Dong-yol's earned run average, 1.28. Well below average.

People often say you have to join the army to become an adult. I'm not sure if this is true. But at least my military days allowed me to reflect on myself as a hard-working online writer. By the time I was a private first class, I had begun to admit that I could not make ends meet simply by writing things that fewer than a hundred people raved about, and by the time I rose to corporal, the popularity of the once hot novels had dampened.

In the summer of that year, the novels lying about the common room were tied together and moved to the waste disposal warehouse ahead of the division commander's visit to the unit. And before the autumn, the world of dragons and magic, chivalry and martial deeds, was sold off by weight by the quartermaster. That was followed by the 1997 IMF crisis. None of us soldiers really knew what the IMF crisis meant. People said it meant that there would be nothing for us to do, even if we got back out into society. Several men in their final year even chose to remain in the military instead of being discharged, which created quite a stir.

By the time I rose to sergeant, rumours had begun to spread among the recruits that the internet was a rising trend. *StarCraft*, Jimmy O. Yang videos and the incomprehensible words 'Red Muffler' were on everyone's lips. As soon as a new recruit arrived, before he could put down his bag, he was asked, 'What the hell is the internet?'

'Just go to a PC room. There's everything there.'

'Is there really loads of good stuff there? That kind of thing, too?'

When a man about to be discharged lying in one corner asked this, twitching his groin, the barracks room fell as quiet as a mouse.

'You can see ab-so-lute-ly every-thing.'

At once, dozens of throats could be heard swallowing hard. Probably the blood went rushing to the same number of cocks. Like those swollen groins, rumours about the internet took on flesh as some kind of myth or legend. For example, there were rumours that the image quality of Red Muffler was so clear that you could see the woman's private parts more clearly than in a cinema.

What was more impossible, wherever there was a computer, the whole world was connected, people who didn't know each other talked on the computer, and a woman's private parts could be seen without being pixelated.

The troops were enthusiastic, but I was nervous. I became even more nervous because I didn't know the reason for my anxiety.

One winter's night when I had some leave ahead of being discharged, I too was sitting in a PC room. I tried to dial in but I couldn't figure out how. I asked the staff and the staff just laughed.

'That's what you do with a phone line. This is LAN, LAN.'

I didn't know what LAN was, and I wasn't feeling motivated to ask any more. I returned home helplessly, searched through my closet, found a modem terminal with the name of the carrier covered in dust, and connected it to a phone line. The connection by modem remained the same. That long dialling sound and the noise. Without realising it, my fingers began to itch.

However, something was wrong with the first connection screen. At the bottom of the screen was a notice that the service would soon be discontinued. And the number of people accessing the noticeboard was incredibly small, only three digits. Even after two years, I hadn't forgotten the shortcuts and pressed quickly to enter the club. The club's last post was from three months ago. Even that had only been read by five people, five people with a lot of regrets for having wasted their time.

I entered the club's bulletin board and began to erase what I had written. I felt that a period in my life was coming to an end. If the club was still crowded, I could have laughed it off, saying, 'That was another time.' But the fact that it was over was very clear. *No*, I was telling myself, *it's been over since goodness knows when, you're behind the times.*

An ordinary life awaited me, one leading to employment, marriage, an increasing salary and fatherhood. It wasn't that I didn't want that kind of life. One night when there was no work in the unit, I even named my first and second children while on guard duty. However, I could not easily accept the fact that my writing days were over, even if fewer than a hundred people enthused over what I wrote.

The next day, I threw away my modem terminal in front of the house. I offered to return it to the company, but they said that I didn't have to. Every time I came home during that vacation, I saw the terminal lying abandoned in front of the gate. No one picked it up. Every time I saw it, I blushed as if I had been caught doing something wrong.

When I returned from vacation, my junior colleagues asked me what Red Muffler was like. I answered, 'What she does with her waist is a work of art. It just made me melt. Melt.'

Snow was melting on the parade ground. I smiled like an accomplice at a private who had returned from vacation a week earlier than I did. The place where the snow had melted was dirty mud, a mixture of soil and snow.

Having been discharged from the army in the spring, I struggled to just *adapt* as they say. When I tried to buy a new beeper, someone told me that I needed to buy a mobile phone, and instead of sitting in a PC room and picking out three-cushion billiards, I learned the shortcut to *StarCraft*. *StarCraft* was very difficult. You didn't have time to think, unlike with billiards. You had to gather maximal resources as fast as possible, then build the most efficient buildings with them, then collect units from them – as well as fighting the most efficient battles. The bottom line was efficiency and economics. It was really a new concept for me. I couldn't believe I had to study to learn how to play.

Then I went online to finish my vacation homework and experienced the new world of the World Wide Web. It would have been a great new world if only it *was* great, but when I took off my military uniform, it was essentially just an expansion of PC communications to a global scale. I also felt somewhat deceived, because the company I applied to for a new internet line was the same company that had offered PC communications before. The fact that PC communications were over didn't mean the companies were doomed. It was just a drop in profits and a discontinuation of services. I took my major classes without missing one, bought a three-colour highlighter and a ruler to organise my notes.

Since the IMF bailout, harrowing rumours of how hard it was to get a job circulated like ghosts among students returning from the army. Some claimed that this year's graduates were all idle, or that one of the graduates from last year had committed suicide. In order to survive I got up at dawn to grab a place in the library, and over lunch I leafed through TOEIC books like crazy, memorising English vocabulary. In the evenings, other returning students and I talked about the difficulty of adapting, downing soju with barbecued chicken ribs, which were no longer all the rage, until we threw up. What boom would come next? We mustn't be late. That in itself would be evidence of maladjustment.

Everyone knew it instinctively. Because that's what we learned in the military. You should never stand out from others, nor should you lag behind. If you don't adapt, you don't survive. Darwin called it survival of the fittest, Adam Smith called it the market, the army called it adaptation and society called it being mature. It was then that someone from the Company came to see me.

* * *

I ran into him at the entrance of an internet cafe near the school gate. In celebration of the end of mid-term exams, I was on my way out after completing an insignificant battle in *StarCraft*'s virtual world with other students back from the army. He was in a piss-smelling alley next to the back gate, in a black suit and gold-rimmed glasses. An ordinary man in his mid-forties, he stood out in an alley like that. He called my name. I stopped and stood there with the polite expression that I would show all the alumni at our reunion years later. Seeing the look on my face, he then called me by my old PC communications username. At that short word, instinctively, I could not help smiling.

He said he was one of my fewer than one hundred fans and had once made a statement at an offline meeting three years before. But I didn't remember. He invited me to go for a drink. There was to be no more lingering over the past. So I had to drink. He would pay for it.

I couldn't help gaping at the sight of the glasses on the long red granite table. Light from halogen lamps was flowing down the walls, the leather sofa was yielding and made me feel strangely warm. I swallowed hard. Suddenly, doubts began to circulate in my head about whether this might not be one of those new fraud schemes involving the price of drinks. My heart was pounding and my mouth grew dry. Fear of maladjustment came over me. I muttered to myself in an attempt to calm down. If it was a scam, he wouldn't have known my name and username. Meanwhile, the man in the black suit called the madam in charge, and a series of young women came in. While I was gawking, he spoke casually.

'Pick one.'

It was my first time in a room salon, so I couldn't understand the situation. Each woman introduced herself briefly. While I looked puzzled, he frowned and told the madam, 'I don't think he likes any of these, let's see some others.'

The madam nodded. The women who had come in went out and another group arrived. Only then did I realise that I was meant to pick one of the ladies who came into the room. So it was a place to choose a woman as if I was picking a product from a vending machine. I felt strange on first encountering this other side of the world, one I didn't know. But at the same time I was afraid. I couldn't imagine the commercial value of that sleek girl in her early or mid-twenties wearing a tight tank top.

Apart from that thought, however, my body was pointing its finger at a woman in a dress with a low back, the top of her buttocks almost showing. The man in the black suit nodded in satisfaction. While the woman sat down and green tea, bottled water, whiskey and beer were laid out one after another on the table in front of us, all kinds of thoughts followed. All of this was an incomprehensible place, an incomprehensible situation and an incomprehensible world for me, whose hair had not yet grown long after wearing it short in the military. I could feel my legs trembling with anxiety that I might be swindled in return for my maladjustment.

The woman sitting next to me whispered, pressing my left arm between her breasts, 'You seem nervous, maybe it's the first time … you've come?'

I nodded. The ensuing laughter tickled the tips of my ears. Confused by the cosy touch that passed across my left arm, my mind grew slightly blank and pale, then blazed hot with passion. Anxiety bleaches things that way. The guy in the black suit gave me a smile, or it might have been a sneer. Now, in retrospect, all this must have been a routine procedure for him. In fact, it was standard for business entertainment in Korea. But for me, who didn't even know about the existence of the Company, and who was still a student, the whole situation was totally strange and unfathomable.

Before I knew it, there was a beer glass in front of me that was holding a small whirlwind, and once I drank it in a single draught, my tension and legs seemed to relax at the same time.

'What was your favourite part in your writing?' the black-suited man asked with a generous expression, suggesting that he could understand everything.

'What …? Why, I don't know.'

'Perhaps your work is more about the process of committing a crime than solving a case. Actually, I think it's more thrilling to commit a crime than to solve a case. People don't understand that very well. That's why I always wanted to meet you and buy you a drink.'

He burst into a cheerful laugh. I laughed along with him. His views on my writing were translated into one English word: *Relax*. My English had improved because I studied TOEIC books hard. I was so proud of myself. At least this didn't seem like a scam. As I relaxed, one hand crept up the thigh of the young lady sitting beside me before I realised. It was just a conditioned reflex, really just an involuntary act, to paw at the inside of that elastic thigh.

After two hours of intermittent conversation, the man said he was in charge of headhunting at a consulting firm. I liked that, I guess. The smell of the perfume of the young woman sitting beside me, her body temperature passing over into my arm and the touch of her breasts was enough. And even in that tense situation, I felt proud of myself for having chosen this lady. I couldn't come back here because even an internet cafe at 1,000 won per hour was a big financial burden for me. So I had to enjoy this time as much as I could. He smiled understandingly as if he knew how I felt.

Before we left the room salon, he called the madam and pulled out a credit card.

'Get the kid ready.'

He gave a sign and the ladies followed the madam out.

To me, puzzled as I was by the incomprehensible situation, he whispered in a low voice, leaning forward, 'Do you remember that piece of writing?'

'Which one do you mean?'

'That short story you posted on the bulletin board about a rich old man who planned and executed a perfect crime against his sons. Do you remember?'

'Yeah, "Total Murder". That went down pretty well on the bulletin board.'

Once I was drunk, I started speaking in a military tone of voice without realising it. I was ashamed that I still didn't seem to have adapted to social life.

'A publisher I'm consulting with these days is planning just that kind of crime novel, and I think you're the perfect writer for it.'

I laughed. 'Wow, that's ridiculous. It wouldn't sell a hundred copies. I don't even remember the last time I wrote ... Surely that kind of thing would never sell?'

'We're the ones who decide whether it will sell or not.'

Yes, he said 'we'. Drunk as I was, I thought that he meant he and I. Had 'we' already decided?

While I was still stammering, he stuck his business card in my jacket pocket. I was embarrassed. 'Write something,' he said.

I had thrown that kind of impulse away, together with my modem. Because it didn't fit with reality. But now the man in the suit in front of me was saying it was possible. He smiled mildly at me in my confusion, encouragingly, as if everything would be fine. Suddenly I wondered how many kinds of smiles he had left. He seemed to know how to speak with just a smile.

While I was trying to refuse, the young lady who had been sitting beside me reappeared, having changed her clothes. She grabbed my elbow and we linked arms. The effect of the alcohol returned, my legs felt weak. I could feel her body pressing tightly against one side of mine. It was so soft, warm and sweet that I felt I was going to melt into her.

'Stand up,' she whispered.

As I rose from my seat, I leaned on the wrong leg, stumbled and buried my face in her breast. She laughed, so I laughed, too.

'Think about it,' the black-suited man said. 'This is a rare opportunity.'

I wanted to say something, but by the time I got my thoughts sorted out, I was in a hotel room. I felt possessed. Once again, the young lady told me not to be nervous. I replied that I wasn't nervous, but it didn't seem to me to make much difference. I felt like I was standing alone in the middle of a sixteen-lane highway with traffic roaring past in both directions. And as I watched the passing cars, I felt as if I was masturbating in the middle of the highway with my genitals exposed. The cars were going too fast and there were too many of them.

That night I failed utterly to cum.

There was only a phone number on the business card I received. No title, no company name, not even the man's name. If the phone number hadn't been silver-coated on a black piece of paper the size of a business card, I might have mistaken it for a bank note instead. And time was a problem. There wasn't really anything to worry about, but I needed time to overcome my fear. What finally cleared my mind was the thought, *This actually is the beginning, you know!* It was only natural to be afraid. However, on reflection, I should have thought about it more. I was naive to think, at the time, that it was a no-lose offer. I had no idea what I was going to do or what it would mean to be cut off from normal life. That would be the last time I had a choice. Of course, there were many choices to make after that, but it was very clear what kind of consequences I would have to endure if I chose differently.

It took me three days to overcome the confusion and fear. Those three days of fear might also have been subject to some judgement by the Company. Now I wonder if the Company was pleased or unhappy that I wavered.

Condominium

Exactly one week later, I was in a condominium in Gangwon Province, near the east coast. I was there to write. It was a biggish condominium in the middle of nowhere, standing empty in a large, deserted car park. It was probably not built as a condo in the first place, it looked more like a tourist hotel or an inn, but it seemed to have been remodelled during the condominium boom in the mid-1990s. The facilities were new, but the carpets and lights were old and it felt dreary.

The day before, the man had said there was no time to lose, I had to start writing right away. If he hadn't pushed me, I wouldn't have gone to such a place, like something from a horror movie, all alone. I'd said, 'What? Right away?' and then intended to continue with, 'But there's a bit of a problem,' but before I had time, he held out a cheque. I could have just read the Korean words written on the cheque but I was so surprised that I counted the number of zeros instead, while he explained that this was the first deposit. I checked the number of zeros twice. He said he needed many episodes in order to produce a whole series. I tried to look embarrassed at this but it didn't work.

'This is a lot of money...'

I had the sudden urge to pee. Seeing my expression, he smiled. 'You're worried that the novel might fail, but you don't have to worry about that.'

'Oh?'

'I'm asking for a thoroughly planned novel.'

'Hmm.'

'The publisher's planning team will provide all the characters, materials and the whole plot. That's all you have to look at. No pressure, none at all.'

He stressed the words 'none at all'. To be honest, I didn't feel good. I also felt a little bit deceived, and I thought I was being looked down on. Still, I was relieved. I was beginning to understand that the so-called publishers were trusting me to write quality novels. Apparently, they were a team of idiots who thought they were smart and that there was going to be a crime novel boom; they were looking for a writer to produce a series of novels at a bargain price, and that writer was me. Since I felt no particular authorial identity, literary ambition or pride as a creator, I didn't feel so bad about this. Suddenly, I wondered if it was too much to say that they would be mass-produced at a bargain price, but I didn't. At that time, I did not know how much novelists were paid and did not want to know. At least, assuming the cheque was not a counterfeit.

I rushed to the bank. The cheque was real. There was no need for any questions. I knew how to act if I received some money. I think I sang a song while packing up. I thought I was masturbating in a sixteen-lane highway, but when I came to my senses, I was driving a Porsche down an empty road.

Around lunchtime the next day, I started to have regrets as I stood in front of the condo. The moment I looked at the building, a short exclamation – 'Hmm, suspicious' – popped out automatically. The car park was empty, and the building seemed to have just been completed or to be on the verge of being demolished. Passing from the outside to the inside, the interior was a mixture of new and old, so I couldn't guess which it really was. The hallway was plastered with purple wallpaper, with navy blue carpets thick enough to make you feel like you were sinking when you stepped on them. Obviously not an interior designed with any normal human sensibility. The lobby's front desk was oddly modern, but the sofa right next to it was antique. Curiously, all of this was quite appropriate. Everything in the condo was like that. What was about to be broken up and what had just been built were like cross-bred, still-born babies. When I asked a member of staff about this, he answered briefly, as with his answers to my other questions, 'This is the way it is in the off season.' I asked several more questions, but the answers were the same. It occurred to me all of a sudden to wonder if this condo was the true meaning of the saying, 'View the old and learn the new.'

The most impressive aspect of the new installations was the internet, which was available even in my own room. At that time, the internet boom was just starting but it was limited to big cities everywhere.

I had whined about the material and coverage right before the man in the suit left. And he had explained that the connection would go all the way to my room. He said there was no need for me to worry because the publishers would be sending materials by email.

Unbelievably, the internet in my room was faster than at home. Something about that felt very unfair. When I got back to Seoul, I would call the company that had betrayed me over my internet connection, I thought while I used the web browser to surf. But it wasn't the internet or the strange appearance of the condo that surprised me the most. There were still a lot of surprises ahead, and my work had only just begun.

The last surprise that day came when I opened the balcony window. Late that evening, when I went out to smoke a final cigarette before going to bed, I heard an owl calling from somewhere. Having been born and raised in a city, it was the first real owl call I'd ever heard. I was appalled by the sound, which I had only ever heard in the television series *Korean Ghost Stories*. The dark forest beyond the car park brought unpleasant images to my mind whenever the wind shook the branches. They would appear and disappear as the wind blew. I sucked in the cigarette smoke rapidly, as if testing the limits of my lung capacity. I felt proud of myself as I saw the red glow approaching the butt in a flash. I was feeling a little dizzy, maybe because I had inhaled too fast. As I breathed out the smoke I looked up to clear my head. The cigarette smoke dispersed in the light streaming out through the balcony door and melted into the darkness. It was a beautiful sight. And it was a strange sight, too. Everything was dark except for the light from the window. I stepped further out onto the balcony, leaned against the railing, stretched out my neck and turned to look at the condo. I stopped breathing for a moment. There was no light visible from any of the balconies or windows. My room was the only one in the whole building with a light on.

Suddenly, I felt as if something was creeping up behind my back. I yanked open the door into the hallway. Both ends of the empty hallway looked exceptionally far away. Along the dark purple walls, the dim light seemed to flow down and stick to the blue carpet. I walked toward the elevators. Even the sound of my footsteps was absorbed by the thick carpet, as if I was walking in a vacuum. My heart pounded as if it was about to explode. I pressed the elevator button desperately.

'Quick, down to the lobby ...'

The elevator was coming up with a sighing sound. But the floor numbers changed slowly, as if they were carved on a stone plaque. Then I realised what I would hear even if I went down to the lobby. *That's the way things are in the off season.*

The elevator door opened. Suddenly, all my actions felt foolish and impulsive. I would simply call them and ask to move somewhere else in the morning. I went back to the room and locked the door. I knew now that there was no one there, but even after checking the door twice, I leaned a chair against the doorknob at an angle so that a potential intruder would be unable to open the door, even if they tried to kick it in.

I woke up several times and thought I heard someone walking down the hallway. But every time I opened the door, there was no one there, only the corridor, empty, plunged in silence.

My request for a change of accommodation was flatly rejected, because there would be no other way for the publisher to send the data. Few hotels even had internet. It turned out that the internet at the condo, which was faster than at home, was actually shackling me. When the man asked why I had to change accommodation, I was at a loss for a reply. I couldn't ask for a different condo just because I was afraid to write where I was. The good news was that the material arrived from the publisher. If I could focus on my work, I would forget my fears.

I checked the data. The material was as amazing as the condominium. He was right. There was no need for me to do any research. Starting with a sketch of the space serving as a background, it included detailed data about the condition of each character, with the results of recent physical check-ups, which might be useful, as well as detailed daily routines of each character. The only thing they didn't send was the actual story.

I so admired the wonderful material that I pinned the outlines of each character and their locations on the wall, so that I could reconstruct their actions, movements and daily lives with pins and colour coding. Then their daily lives came close, near enough to touch. Each had some ambiguity, but not enough to affect the writing of the novel. On the contrary, I was worried that too much data might restrict my imagination.

However, what I couldn't understand was that even though the data for the minor characters was so detailed, there was little information about the main character. When the man phoned to check that I had received the data, I asked about this and he replied, 'Surely the main character should be left to the writer's freedom?' He asked me to create an anti-hero who would combine Professor Moriarty, Holmes's arch-rival, and Norton, the arch-villain who could only die when Poirot did. What the publisher wanted was a series featuring an attractive behind-the-scenes mastermind. The series even had a grand title, *Master of Puppets*. They wanted a dark hero who would bring secret death to wicked people who were never punished by the law.

Master of Puppets

Master of Puppets is the title of Metallica's third album released in 1986. On the cover of the album, a large red hand hovers over a graveyard lined with white crosses, and from the red hand dangle white threads that control puppet-like cross-shaped tombstones. The cover is as impressive as the songs on the album. The title track of the same name, 'Master of Puppets', sings about the lives of addicts who are caught up in drugs and manipulated like puppets. If you look at the lyrics of this song, you can clearly see how dominance is achieved. It is made up of fantasy and addiction, fear and command. This became Metallica's signature song and put the band on top of the world in an instant. It also became my soundtrack while I wrote.

The car park smelled faintly of paint. He glanced in the rear-view mirror. There was no one else in the car park. He opened the glovebox. There was a syringe inside. He skilfully filled the syringe with insulin. Maybe it was because he took the insulin by himself, he reckoned he was used to giving himself injections by now. It had always been hard to handle syringes with his awkward hands. The syringe was terribly small in his fingers.

He hated his hands. His father had hands like that, too. He had been hit a lot with those hands. Farmer's hands. His father was a typical farmer who always said that caterpillars had to feed on pine beetles. But he didn't like that kind of defeatism. He thought of how caterpillars fly when they emerge from their cocoons. Ever since he started ploughing fields along the slopes of mountains, he knew that he would not end up just as a pine beetle and did everything he could to make it so. Some might curse at such a life. But that would just be an excuse for losers. After all, 'the value of anything must be judged on its results', and all is well that ends well. He smiled. Now he was obliged to take all responsibility. He would fight to the bitter end. He had always been like this. He had never stepped down from a fight since he'd been digging for potatoes in Gangwon Province. It didn't matter who his opponent was. He ran at them like a dog and bit until they fell down. Although now he wore a suit and drove a foreign car, and was honoured with the title of Secretary General, his nature had not changed. With these hands inherited from a farmer, he only had to smash mercilessly.

He bowed his head. The hand holding the syringe caught his eye. The hand looked strangely small. As if his hands were shrinking.

'I must be getting old!'

He clenched his other hand and punched it forward. But he wasn't past fighting yet. He hadn't devoted himself to the party for thirty years just to end up a lizard's tail. He still had the last card. He would hold a press conference the next day. Then it would be clear that it was the party leadership that was running out of fire. There would be no more avoiding contacting him, like now. No. Rather, the others would be burning to contact him. He enjoyed just imagining it. Then he would come to an agreement with the party leadership about how to deal with the ones who had abandoned him and fled like rats. Their demands were obvious, and he didn't mean to refuse. There was no way out. He would pretend to step down and take responsibility to some extent. Public opinion should be put to rest. But he would be able to return to his original position before the next election. Certainly, his original position had been weak. He had so many supporters that he was sure of being reinstated even if there was a list of alternative candidates on the table. Just imagining it made him smile.

He undid his dress shirt and grabbed his belly, then stuck the syringe in. He felt a tingling pain and cringed at the cold insulin entering subcutaneous fat. It was odd. He had always been injecting in this way but it was the first time he had had this feeling. Clearly he had made a mistake while he was imagining useless things, like a fool. It was evidence that he was weakening.

He looked ugly sitting in the underground car park like this. Until recently, he had been using a fountain pen-type syringe for his insulin shots in the office. But about a month before, a new employee had noticed what the fountain pen was for. He had tried to cover it up, so then he started giving himself insulin injections in the car park.

What would happen if people learned that he was diabetic? Perhaps youngsters in the opposition would come rushing in after his constituency like hyenas, and not only that, men from other factions would also come stampeding. His juniors were no different. He considered himself an easy-going old man but this was by no means the end of his ambitions. Everyone might think he was a lucky hillbilly who had somehow managed to make it all the way up here. It was good to put them off their guard, but they shouldn't be allowed to trample him down. In the jungle, the first to become prey are the old and sick animals. So he wouldn't have any of the things a diabetic had to carry about.

His blood glucose monitor stayed hidden in his drawer. He only measured his blood sugar before going to bed and before going to work. It was a secret that he and his wife alone knew. Carrying sweets, chocolate and juice would be tantamount to advertising that he was diabetic and that was why he came down to the underground car park every day to inject himself with insulin. Sometimes he had a drink, if necessary. The doctor said this was no different than suicide, but he had to take that risk if he was to rise yet higher. Even his driver didn't know he was diabetic. So he changed the glovebox lock and carried the key with him.

He put the empty syringe back in the glovebox and fastened his shirt. Perhaps because it was an underground car park, the September air felt quite chilly. He looked around outside the window. There was no one else in the car park. He was always nervous at this moment. What would he say if he ran into someone he knew? He had been down here so often. He opened the door with trembling hands. Halfway out, he looked around again. As expected, there was not a sound to be heard. He got out of the car completely, coughed, then closed the door. It was incredible. His heart was beating so fast! It hadn't beat like this when he carried apple boxes stuffed with money during the elections. He couldn't deny that he was old now. Suddenly an idea struck him. But he shook his head to get rid of such thoughts. Maybe it was because he thought too much that he felt as if his head was pounding.

He poked a hand into his pocket and started walking toward the elevator. The hand in his pocket kept shaking. At the same time his legs felt weak, as if he had been drinking. His footsteps sounded strange, as if his ears were numb. How many things he could have done if he were only ten years younger. He looked pathetic to himself. His eyesight was growing blurred. He rubbed his eyes, but it didn't help. Suddenly, an ominous thought crossed his mind.

'This ... this ...'

Slow, long sounds. It was beyond belief. He had never been like this in the past four years. When he was first diagnosed with diabetes, he had been told these were signs that a hypoglycaemic shock was approaching, but he had paid little attention. He had to ask someone for help. But there was no one to be seen in the empty underground car park.

'If I can get to the elevator quickly ...'

But just then he felt one knee buckle helplessly. There was a twitching in the middle of his body. There was no doubt about it. He was suffering insulin shock. He couldn't understand. He had injected the exact dose. How come ...?

But there was no time to argue about it. He would die if he didn't get sugar right now or if someone didn't find him. He should have carried sweets around with him. He felt a lot of regrets. Sweets loomed before his fading gaze. Now he could see nothing. He knitted his brows. There were sweets in the box under the handbrake in the car parked right next to him. He realised it wasn't an illusion, it was real.

He slipped between the parked cars, then used all his remaining strength to hit the driver's window. His farmer's hands, which he hated so much, were his only hope of breaking the glass and being saved. But after a few desperate punches, he realised that his body was failing. While he did not have much blood sugar left, it was being wasted on uncovering sweets from behind a window. He couldn't believe he was dying like this in a violent convulsion. There was still too much left to do. It wasn't supposed to end like this. He never dreamed that he would die this way when he left Gangwon Province.

He struggled not to lose hold of his fading string of consciousness. At that moment, he heard someone's footsteps. It was obvious that someone would find him. They would see him convulsing and call an ambulance, if they were not stupid. Then he might be hospitalised for a few weeks, but then, again ... In his final moments of fading consciousness, he suddenly realised that he could no longer hear footsteps.

M stopped. He knew he'd be on CCTV if he walked any further.

Stupid guy. He didn't think anyone would know if he hid his disease yet the scene of him giving himself insulin injections had been captured a dozen or more times by the surveillance cameras. Actually, M didn't even need cameras. Just by looking at his credit card record, anyone could see that he had bought insulin every month. M thought: *What easy prey is a human being who believes he is strong.*

His convulsions were abating. Now his body was moving on to the next stage. The brain, having lost its source of energy, glucose, was slowly trying to stop working. If he had fallen in the middle of the car park, he would have been easier to spot. That's why M had prepared a car with sweets in sight.

M felt a little relieved. It was a plan he had spent a month concocting. Over the past month, the syringe had gradually been growing larger, insensibly. That was why it was becoming easier to inject. Of course, the amount of medicine remained unchanged. That was at the heart of the plan.

A month later, the syringe he used was already much larger and thicker than before. But the long period of time had left him completely oblivious to the changes in the syringe. And he had injected the last syringe today. It had an internal diameter that fitted the external size. He had administered nearly four times the amount he should have taken. And so taken his own life. M was curious. Would the police conclude that his death was suicide or an accident?

Soon the security guard and the janitor would be arriving, since the drain was backflowing by now. Of course someone might still find him. But unless he was in front of their car, most people wouldn't care about someone lying in an underground car park for an unknown reason. In the meantime, his brain, having lost its energy source, would slowly begin to die of necrosis. Maybe if he was lucky enough, he might be found by someone and declared brain-dead. Maybe he'd do something good for the first time in his life.

M smiled as he looked at the heavy body, motionless beside the car, and got up from his seat. Ironically, to hide his diabetes, he always pulled into the most deserted part of the car park. And now that prudence was zeroing his chances of recovery. But he also needed to know. Smarter than others, sufficiently mean, moderately powerful, he could escape from any responsibility. But death was not like that. M whistled one last time. The sound rang through the desolate underground car park. Somewhere upstairs, he heard a car climbing toward the exit. As if someone's soul was escaping from their body.

And so I posted off the story I had written to the very address that I would be using countless times in the future.

The first story took me about four weeks, then I was given a week's rest.

I wanted to go up to Seoul, but he opposed it. He brought me any necessities I'd need, and claimed that I had just begun to get into the flow so that the flow would be interrupted if I returned to the regular world. Inwardly I shouted *Nonsense!* but when he placed another cheque in front of me, his argument began to sound reasonable. The idea that I could recover by communing with nature for a week changed to a conviction before the number of zeros of the sum I already knew but found exciting to count again.

I went to the nearby town with him, deposited the money in the bank and came back to the condo, thinking that everything was fine. But I soon started to regret not going to Seoul. There was nothing to do here. All I had was a computer and the internet.

What would you do in an isolated space with no one but an employee who repeats 'It's the off season' like an answering machine? I downloaded videos. What I usually watched was a very leisurely kind of Japanese costumed porno. Indeed, the development of the internet had a remarkably exciting effect on my cock. Adult videos had long been praised as a sign of Japan's advanced or forward-looking culture, and once again I was thrilled by the wide range of actresses – the male actors all looked alike. Now I can barely remember the faces of many of the actresses, but if by chance I met one of the male actors on the street, I'd be able to recognise him at once. So I spent a week amazed at the depths of various perverted tastes. It was a lonely week, with no company but a roll of tissue and a right hand. The cum, which flowed all week long, was phenomenal by the end. I suddenly wanted to write like crazy.

A new batch of data arrived, as if he could read my mind. But it was different from the last time. The main character was a church pastor. Not only did he have no chronic disease, but he had no time to be alone. He was busy from Monday to Sunday, there were so many visits to make and events to attend. Seeing that, my prejudice collapsed, for I had thought that pastors only had to work on Sundays.

Despite his busy schedule, he had a mistress. On weekdays, he and a deaconess working in his church would meet at a motel and spend time together. Suddenly, I felt an urge to murder him. The distinction between virtual and real life was no longer important to me, having spent a week with a roll of paper and lovers on a monitor. Moreover, although he was a pastor, he had a doctor and received thorough health care. A pastor with his own doctor, it was incredible! It seemed almost impossible to kill him off when he had no time alone, no serious illness and a doctor in tow.

It was only after three days of gloom and jealousy that I suddenly realised that the pastor was not a real person. There was no reason for me to be jealous. After rolling about on the floor and laughing at myself, almost in tears, I started from scratch. Beginning from the end, I designed the most perfect ending by reconstructing his death. It sounds pretty easy, but it's a kind of trick. Assuming that he died, I started by finding which death would seem the most natural, then I'd go on to produce the most logical result.

Once I had the materials about his personal life pinned to the wall, I imagined all kinds of ways for him to die. Each of them proved to have a problem. Almost always it was the doctor who was the problem, since the surest enemy of a natural death is an autopsy. Moreover, the pastor had a comprehensive health record. I was angry, but I couldn't change the set-up just because I was stuck. In addition, the pastor was known to be a cautious and attentive character. I couldn't seem to find any weakness other than the illicit liaison, and he was such a careful human being that he would never let anyone know his secret. Perhaps there had been other women from the church who had been involved with him before. But the fact that he boasted a spotless career without any scandals was a good indication of how prudent he was.

I spent two more days at a loss. I introduced the characters and completed their entanglements, but made no further progress.

I spent a few more days feeling as if I was being increasingly hemmed in on every side. The publishing company's planning team must surely be testing my ability, otherwise, there was no reason to impose such an unreasonable setting. The life patterns were making less and less sense.

One day, emerging from the toilet, I looked at my face in the mirror. I thought I was looking quite disgraceful with greasy hair that I hadn't washed for a few days and a scruffy beard. I realised something at that moment. Sometimes there are things that people fear more than death: like shame. He was a minister. It didn't matter if it wasn't a natural death. If it was a death that they wanted to hide, the living would turn it into a natural death. Our actions are determined by our desires, and we have a desire-based orientation. Like in the lyrics of 'Master of Puppets', manipulation is not difficult if you know desire and fear.

From that point on it was full speed ahead. I sat in front of the computer and tapped on the keyboard. There was no time to lose. I had to hurry up and finish the story if I was ever to get out of this awful condo.

It's a very simple story. There was once a pastor. During a home visit, he heard a new church member tell a joke about a man who clung to an external air conditioning unit to escape from a husband who'd returned home unexpectedly while the man was enjoying himself with his wife. The pastor thought badly of the new believer for his immoral joke, but everyone else laughed. The rest was like dominoes falling down, one after another. A phone call was made to the husband of the pastor's mistress, informing him about his wife's affair. The husband was full of doubt but came and knocked on the door of the motel room where they were together. The minister was taken by surprise, but he remembered the story he'd heard. The danger of hanging in the air was less significant for him than his honour. Outside the window was a rusty air conditioning unit and he knew he had no choice.

But the ending of the story was a little different from the joke the pastor had heard. Even with faith as strong as an iron fortress, the cement ground below the eleventh floor was too hard to cushion his fall together with the air con unit. His doctor wrote a medical certificate blaming overwork for the pastor's death, thereby saving his honour. He wasn't wrong. Hanging on to an outdoor air con unit on the eleventh floor would be exhausting work for anyone. All the more so if the bolts holding it up were rusty.

The man came after a month and a half away, bringing a change of clothes. I begged him to let me go home and rest. I didn't care about money or anything else. He assured me that he would give me a good break for about two months if I wrote one more episode. But that in itself was not enough. He was well aware of this fact, too. He held out a cheque for about twice the amount I had received previously, saying that he was very satisfied with my last story. I could feel my hand shaking as I accepted it. What more could I say? He flashed the benevolent smile I had seen at the room salon. I smiled back. Suddenly, I felt unbearably servile. But what use is a noble life?

I couldn't go to Seoul so I went to Chuncheon instead. Walking along streets that stank of sewers, I felt a pure passion that had been acutely trained in the empty condo. Turning the corner of an alley I came across a crowd of soldiers. Their eyes were bloodshot, their shoelaces half untied and their shirts sticking out over their combat trousers. And there were faces visible through windows, faces with red light falling on them. From somewhere, I heard the sound of a train's whistle. I buried my face in a breast and cried like a pop song. I still don't know what kind of tears they were.

The main character in the last story was different from the previous two. He was such an easy target. There were no obstacles, no safeguards to prevent his death. It was inevitable because he couldn't have been more wretched. It was odd. He was a farmer in his mid-sixties, too humble to be anyone's enemy. He was so unassuming that he had never even taken part in the village's annual relay race. There were early signs of various adult diseases, and he was in bad health, because the two packs of cigarettes he took with him every morning, and the three bottles of soju he got through at home every evening, were his only pleasures in life. Killing him wasn't a problem, but no matter how hard I thought about it, there was simply no reason for anyone to kill him. The victims of the previous two stories had moral problems, and their lives were intertwined with other people's interests. Therefore, their deaths were convincing enough. But this guy didn't have anything like that. His house was merely a half-collapsing cement building from the time of the Saemaul Movement; then he had borrowed money from the National Agricultural Cooperative Federation to build a pigsty, and all he owned was fifteen pigs.

Who in the world would want to kill such a humble human being? If someone has to be killed, there must be a corresponding price. So the victims of hit-and-run murders are mainly the rich. Who on earth would want to kill a farmer whose only wealth was fifteen pigs? I couldn't think of a reason. I suddenly realised that this was a new assignment from the planning team, a test to see how interesting a novel I could write with such a character.

I reconstructed the life of the farmer. Why was he living alone? That meant there was something secret about him. As I looked at his record again, step by step, Vietnam attracted my attention. He must have done something there, because past sins never let go of us.

I created a virtual survivor, a boy in a village. The farmer had committed an appalling atrocity in Vietnam, and the boy had been the only survivor. Then the farmer, who thought the villagers were all dead, returned to his home-town and began farming again. Meanwhile, the boy lived a miserable life but never forgot the man who drove him to the brink, who summoned the villagers then blew them all up together.

The boy sometimes dreams of that night even after he becomes an adult. It's not long before he gets a chance. At the end of the Cold War, after the Soviet Union collapsed and Vietnam reformed and opened up, he had raised money by fair means and foul, only for revenge. The boy, now middle-aged, has been waiting for so long. He hires someone with the money he's amassed. That person decides to kill the farmer in the same way he killed the villagers, as his client asks.

I wrote about an absurd, bizarre death. It was so strange that it seemed like a lie, yet I created a death that could only be considered an accident.

That was the last piece of rubbish I wrote. The reason I call it that is simple. In fact, it didn't have to be so long or have so many characters. I agonised over minor relationships and settings for several days, but they were all superfluous. The only thing needed was the death itself. I read and corrected the story three times to make proper sentences, but it was no different from putting rubbish in a washing machine and turning it on. Rubbish is rubbish, whether you wash it or not, after all.

Sometimes I miss that moment. It was a really lonely and terrible moment, but somehow it was full of dreams, too. I really believed my works were going to be published, in a naive way.

The last time I saw the condo it didn't look as bleak as the first time. I had got used to being alone, so that I ran around the empty corridors naked and stomped about, dancing all night. It was only on that first day that I'd heard strange sounds. There were no more surprises for me in the condo. But I was a little sad that I had to leave just as I was getting used to it. Would the peak season ever come?

The man turned his head as the car was leaving and asked me if I felt sorry to see the back of the condo. I said no, I had just thought it was an amazing place at first but now I didn't think so. He laughed.

But that was not the end. It was much later that the condominium revealed its biggest surprise. A few years later, I happened to pass in front of it and drove into the car park, thinking of the old days. The condo was completely ruined and devastated. The glass door leading to the lobby was shattered, the cement was peeling in places and the carpets were covered with dust as thick as time. I turned the car and was driving out of the condo when I spotted a farmer driving a cultivator in front of me.

'When did this condo fail?' I asked.

'It's never been in business. It went bankrupt in the IMF crisis just before it opened, so it couldn't even start up. It's been that way ever since.'

I broke out in a cold sweat. So it was a ruined place when I was rolling on the floor like a dog. That's why the interior was so weird. Maybe if I didn't know what the Company was, I would remember this as a ghost story. I spent four months in a condo that never opened.

So I came back to Seoul. He dropped me off in front of my home and told me I had worked hard. I took a deep breath.

'This polluted air makes me feel alive. The smell of freedom is strong.'

He laughed loudly and said, 'Freedom, that's fine. You feel that way because you've been working hard. Why, there's a saying: Labour sets you free.'

That's how he left. That was the last time I saw him. 'Labour sets you free.' It was a phrase that I had heard somewhere, but I couldn't remember where. A few months later, I read in a magazine that the Bible says, 'The truth will set you free.' I thought perhaps he had misquoted that phrase. But he hadn't, of course.

A few years later, late one night, I was planning the murder of a wealthy eighty-year-old grandmother. She had lived too long, and her grandson was impatient. In the meantime, his parents had died and he was the only heir, such a common case. There was a documentary on the channel I always switched on when I came home, and I heard an actor's voice saying, 'Labour sets you free.' I stopped what I was doing and ran in front of the TV. On the screen was a black-and-white photograph of a group of people walking through an arched door into a brick building. Perhaps the German words written on the arch-shaped gate meant, 'Labour sets you free.' I stood there blankly and watched the documentary. The explanation for the picture emerged. The photograph showed Jews heading into a gas chamber. It was Auschwitz.

Evidence

I was happy for just two months. My bank account contained enough money to buy a small house. I left university as if I had been kidnapped. My grades were a disaster, but it didn't matter, I was a writer now. But happiness is always half supported by anxiety. Would the books really sell when they came out? Suppose the publisher gave up on the plan and demanded the money back, what should I do then?

In fact, I knew the reason for my anxiety. I kept hearing this voice from a corner of my heart: *This can't be happening. No publishing company entrusts a young writer with a whole series of novels. Especially not crime stories.* Every time I heard this voice I went to the bank and checked my balance. Only the amount in my account proved that I had been locked up writing for a while in a strange condo.

Instinct was warning me that something was off, that this wasn't normal. So I didn't let anyone know what I'd been doing. My friends asked me where I had been. I replied that I'd been on a language training course. Around that time, there was a boom in language training. No one even asked me anything more because they were too busy talking about the time they had spent abroad. I acted like a gambler in a casino holding a royal straight flush. I pretended to be worried about getting a job, and as though keeping up with classes was too much for me. For two months, people kept looking into my face and asking if I was having a hard time. Every time I would look away, sigh and reply: 'That's life.'

Two months later, I started to get nervous. He had told me to take a break for about two months but I couldn't think of anything else when I woke up in the mornings, wondering if he had meant exactly two months, or two months and twenty-nine days, or if I should call first.

I went to school with the intention of waiting just one more day. I was sitting with my TOEIC book open, but I couldn't see the words. There were more things to forget than English words to be memorised. I couldn't stand it, so I went down to the reading room and looked at the newspapers.

I was sitting there with a bound bundle of news from the past month, but I was only half absorbed. As the print crumbled then came together again, I kept wondering what was wrong with my head. Just then, a small article loomed through the crumbling type at the bottom of the general news page. Church, pastor, air conditioner, dead. I turned to the next page, scanned some other articles, then thought: *What was that?* As soon as I turned back, the title caught my eye.

Overwork death of famous pastor caused by fall.

All of a sudden, I laughed out loud. The people in the reading room were all staring at me. I got up, leaving the newspapers where they were, and headed for the door. In front of the exit I stopped and thought: *No, it can't be.* But my arm was already pulling out the bundle of the previous month's newspapers. It must have been a coincidence. Back at my desk, I turned over the papers at a rapid pace. Someone touched my shoulder. Surprised, I dropped my bag on the desk with a loud clatter.

The girl sitting next to me murmured with a look of surprise, 'Could you please turn the pages over quietly?'

I bowed my head, said sorry and picked up the bag. I took a deep breath and skimmed through the newspaper again, beginning to read the articles meticulously. It was right there. The article about the ruling party's former Secretary General who had died of chronic diabetes. Apparently, his death was likely to leave the investigation into political funds at a standstill.

With every heartbeat, my head seemed to be splitting, my heart was leaping like a locust in a frying pan. I came out of the library. It must have been a coincidence. Every year, many politicians and pastors die. It didn't matter at all. It was all just a coincidence. As I walked back home my legs trembled. A friend called my name in front of the PC room, but I couldn't reply. I went home, pulled a blanket over my head and fell asleep without eating dinner. I really needed to sleep.

When I opened my eyes, it was already past midnight and I was hungry. I opened the refrigerator. None of the snacks were edible. I took out some milk, went to the living room and turned on the TV. The reporter on the screen was standing in front of a cement building where marks of a fire were still visible.

'It's like a battlefield.'

It really was almost like a battlefield. There was a burnt cement building, its roof blown off, and burnt pig carcasses. I dropped the carton I was holding and the milk spilled out.

'Police suspect that methane gas accumulating in the manure tank under the pigsty exploded after a burning cigarette was thrown away by Mr Kim.

Along the living-room wall, the light from the TV wavered. I could recall the missing part of the half-collapsed building. I'd seen the blueprint of the cross section.

'Meanwhile, Mr Kim was taken to hospital with burns all over his body, but he died within two hours.'

Yes, the explosion was important. For the boy in the novel, it was revenge. In my novel, the farmer had gathered the villagers in one place and asked the US for an air strike. Napalm had poured down on them like rain. Of course, that much had been my creation. I could feel cold milk slowly oozing between my toes. I looked down and stared for a moment at the white puddle on the floor.

'What happened?' I muttered. 'It's a coincidence.'

I knew that cigarette butts didn't accidentally fall into manure tanks filled with methane gas, causing accidental explosions, leading to accidental deaths. Maybe, if someone was terribly unlucky, that could happen. But the chances of the pigsty that was the site of the explosion being exactly the same as the cross section in my publishing material, and the exact number of fifteen pigs being the same, were as remote as winning a lottery several times. Nevertheless, I kept muttering, 'Surely it's a coincidence.'

The news changed. The footage showed an overturned truck, black oil running over the ground. I felt something cold and slippery between my toes. Looking down, I remembered the milk that had escaped from the milk carton. I fetched a mop and as I wiped the floor I thought about what I'd done. For goodness' sake, I had let the whole carton of milk spill till it was empty. It didn't matter. Anger rose belatedly. I had been used. I threw the mop aside and picked up the phone. I had to call the police. But as I pressed the number I stopped. What would I tell them? I could explain things as they were. I was about to dial the number again when I thought of what I would say. *There's been a murder, but it looks like an accident, but I actually planned it, though I didn't plan it, I didn't mean to, and I don't know who was behind it, but...*

As my excitement subsided, the hand holding the phone grew weak. It was clear that the police wouldn't believe anything I said. It sounded like crap even to me. And suppose someone did believe it, there was no evidence. I had planned the murder so brilliantly, there was no witness nor even a scrap of evidence. I had been in the condo the whole time I was working. Suddenly, I realised that this was why I had been kept shut up in such an unconventional space.

Maybe one of the cops might hear me out. Then he'd make a call to a nearby mental hospital. And I'd end up taking medicine at every meal while I wondered: *Did it really happen or was it just an illusion? Did the condo even exist?* My hands were shaking. It didn't really matter at all. After I reported it, would they just stay put? If they killed three people, there was no reason for them not to kill a fourth. I could have acted like the main character in a movie, but there was too much at stake to play an imma-ture hero. I sat down in front of the mop again. I had wiped up all the milk, but the living room with the lights off still smelled of it.

The next day was a day like any other. The next day after that, too. I didn't read the newspapers; I didn't watch the TV news. Strangely, studying went well, and I found I was able to memorise English words. I observed myself and my surroundings carefully. All seemed no different than usual except for a few minor details. I decided to think I was being oversensitive. I wanted to believe that so badly that it really seemed to be the case. After a week, I managed to get a vague picture of what kind of state I was in. I called him. The phone number was out of service. Just as I expected.

After dinner, I went for a walk. I opened my bank book while smoking on a bench in front of a local supermarket. It wasn't a dream. I wonder what might have happened if the police had asked to track my account then. At that time, I didn't know why I hadn't thought about it – was it because I was embarrassed, or because I needed to escape that I was reluctant to give up the money? Of course, it would not have been much evidence either. I had deposited the cheques, but I didn't know where they had come from. Even if the police miraculously believed me and tracked down the money, they'd probably lose the thread at some point. Money laundering must be easier than killing people. I stubbed out the cigarette and got up from the bench. I walked toward my house. As I passed the front gate I knocked on the window of a black car that I had seen parked in front of the house and in front of school all week. I recognised the car because of the number 2415, a number I can still remember even now.

Anyway, the window went down. There was a man in his mid-thirties inside. I'd never seen him before, but the arms bulging beneath his black suit gave me an idea of his job. He looked puzzled, in spite of the intimidating impression he gave off. It was a bit funny because everything from his facial expression to his dress was clumsy.

'Tell him,' I said.

'Eh?'

'I want to talk to him.'

'What ...'

'Just tell him that.'

'No, what ...'

I turned and went toward the house. I could feel his gaze on my back. Before I went inside, I looked round and saw that the car had vanished. I got a text message exactly an hour later.

> You passed the test. Please decide whether to continue working or not and let me know.

Together with a date, time and place. If I knew, that was enough for them. The Company did not talk to individuals. They just gave instructions.

The day before the appointment, I went down to the village where the farmer on the news had lived. At the entrance to the village, estate agents in tents were selling occupancy rights. It didn't take long to learn that the pigsty had been on the planned site of a new city shopping mall. The old farmer didn't want to relocate. It had nothing to do with the Vietnam War. He lived alone because he didn't have enough money to go to Vietnam or some other Southeast Asian country to get himself a wife. To hell with the Vietnam War! I blushed with shame, guilt and anger.

'I couldn't help it, I couldn't help it,' I muttered on my way home.

At last I understood what I was up against. I came back home and deleted what I had written. I couldn't make another choice. I already knew too much, and I was in too deep. I don't know if this was really true. But at least that's what I believed at the time. After the appointment was fixed like that, I met my Manager for the first time at a cafe.

The text message on the mobile phone said I had passed. But the Company didn't tell me the whole story. There were some important words omitted. It took me quite a long time to realise that.

Customers or Clients

I call the people who provide the occasion for my services 'customers'. My 'clients' are the people who give me the job. I don't feel much for any of them. Emotions are the product of some kind of interaction. But neither customers nor clients have any kind of interaction with me. They always exist behind the data as mathematical and inconsequential figures.

At first, when I was a consulting rookie and worried about my conscience, I used to look for a good reason as to why my customer should die. Perhaps I wanted to justify my work. Of course, in the bulky documentation the Company sent, there was nothing about good reasons for the customer's death. However, based on the data they'd send, if I examined it carefully for half a day, I might be able to uncover a reason why the person deserved to die. To be honest, I've never spent more than three hours trying to find a reason for any of my customers to die.

Gap was my fifth customer. He was a manager for a foreign fund company that everyone knows by name, but jumped into the futures market one year and made a record profit. The most interesting thing that year was corn. As the El

Niño phenomenon caused cold sea water to rise, corn prices soared, and so the value of the corn he bought soared, too. It was sub-Saharan Africa, which was parched due to drought, that was most directly hit by the rising price of corn. Hundreds of thousands of people died of starvation. Refugees crossed borders to escape starvation and drought, and in that death march toward refugee camps, the elderly and the weak fell, one after another. International organisations tried to buy food for the refugees, but very little was available because our customer's group had already cornered the futures market.

Corn prices soared further as international organisations jumped in. Africa was not the only place that fell into an abyss. That year, unlike corn, coffee, which had not received much attention in the futures market, plunged. And so other southern hemisphere regions that sold coffee to buy corn suffered, too.

What's really interesting is that Gap never actually had or saw any corn, not even at the last minute when he was selling it. He'd bought corn that didn't exist yet, and sold it without harvesting it. He even sold corn that hadn't sprouted from the ground yet.

Funnier still, he hadn't even used his own money to make his so-called investments. He made a fortune by buying corn that didn't exist with money that wasn't his. Within an imaginary world, he undertook imaginary procedures to trade imaginary images and dominated imaginary realities to create real wealth and real death. Who said it was impossible to create something out of nothing?

Hundreds of people starved to death on account of Gap's lucrative investments. In poor countries, his profit margins and the mortality rate due to starvation increased in similar proportions. I am not a sentimental person. If it wasn't him, someone else would have cornered the market in the name of investment and racked up record returns. He was just a little bit quicker off the mark. But does that mean he could justify the result of his actions? He made a clean sweep of more lives than Hitler or Stalin with just a few mouse clicks and some figures keyed in. Some people call that efficiency. How primitive and inefficient are tanks, bombers, cannons, guns, Siberian prison camps and gas chambers! With his profits, he bought a new car, paid off his credit card debt and gave huge bonuses to the companies and investors who had trusted him. These were transformed into real estate for some, mink coats for others, golf club memberships for others still. Nice shot, boss! That was not all. By dragging out labour-management negotiations, the employees of subcontracting firms were thrown out into the street and there was one union leader who was driven to kill himself and his whole family.

My eighth client, the president of a bank, had lobbied to cash in a South American bond. As a result, the country's health budget was slashed and hundreds of children in the slums died of cholera. This is what is known as a butterfly effect.

I hope you don't misunderstand. These are by no means vicious people, not the usual psychopaths, not the typical money-grubbing guys that come to mind when we think of the super-rich. They were all capable individuals and good neighbours.

Gap, who slaughtered as many people as Hitler did, also donated money to charities that were fighting against global hunger and malnutrition. Of course, he didn't suffer any loss because those sums were tax-deductible. Nevertheless, he couldn't just pass by when he saw people in need. He was a patriot who shed tears on hearing the national anthem, and he was willing to take trouble for the sake of others. Strictly speaking, those deaths were not his fault. But if such a thing is called speaking strictly, in my case I too should not be held accountable, 'strictly speaking'. And 'strictly speaking', no one's death is ever anyone else's fault.

By the time I began planning my tenth murder, I had stopped looking for reasons why my customers should die. It was a waste of time. Everyone had a good reason to die. The term 'pangs of conscience' was just plain superfluous.

Compared to customers, clients have never interested me. Clients were just a source of income, compared with the thorough analysis of the customer that I needed to determine to provide my services. In principle, I couldn't tell who the clients were. However, it was not difficult to guess the client based on the vast amount of customer data they provided. Usually, clients were the people who would benefit the most from the death of a customer. As for me, it was better not to know, so long as they paid me properly. But just once, I met a customer in person.

He was a regular. Or, to be exact, his company was the Company's biggest client. For safety reasons, I cannot go into details but the client – the Chairman's company – was one of the top twenty listed companies and was a conglomerate with many subsidiaries. The customer – the Chairman, that is – knew how to dominate in competition and did everything he could to win, by fair means or foul. Without going into details, he was a regular client for the Company. He was someone who got what he wanted even if it meant killing. He lived in a different world from me, convinced as he was that he was naturally entitled to dominate others. Then the Chairman suddenly started to believe that he needed me, and his tenacity was embodied in the form of a black German saloon parked in front of my house.

'You're Mr XX, right?'

In movies, the messengers of high-up people are always two big men wearing sunglasses and black suits, broad-shouldered guys with low voices. In my case, however, it was a beautiful woman in her late twenties in a dark navy skirt suit. To give my personal opinion, I think that this counterpart was softer, more natural and more efficient than the film version. The secretary with her slightly cold expression reminded me of my Manager somehow. Even before checking her business card, I could guess her job at a glance from her uniquely polite and stiff tone. She handed me a business card that read 'Secretariat'.

'How can I help you?'

'The Chairman would like to see you.'

I followed along meekly because the amazing curve running from her waist to her buttocks told me to. It was much more convincing than the fists of the broad-shouldered guys in the movies. Of course, the name of the company on her business card and the rumours about the world related to that company helped push me along.

The saloon went gliding along the highway until we arrived at a place that was not the Chairman's office in the headquarters building. The German saloon, like a Dobermann, ejected me in a disabled parking area on the lowest level of the underground car park of a new high-rise building in a new satellite city where real estate offices still remained active.

'Follow me.'

I followed the skirt suit wordlessly, my eyes fixed on the secretary's buttocks, the silhouette of which was revealed clearly, and I imagined that the buttocks might somehow represent the Chairman's company. Words like 'breathtaking surplus' and 'hot blue-chips' came meaninglessly to my mind.

She stopped in front of an elevator located beyond two doors with signs that read: 'No access except for authorised personnel.' It was the end of the naive days when I believed that behind such doors there was sure to be nothing but machine rooms. There were no buttons in front of the elevator. The secretary put a key in a keyhole and turned it. The door slid open. She motioned to me to get in. I boarded the elevator with an awkward expression. There were no floor buttons inside the gold elevator, which looked rather like a safe. It was an elevator for only one person, which stopped on only one floor.

The secretary spoke apologetically. 'The Chairman said he wanted to see you alone. Even I can't enter that room easily. It's his private room.'

I smiled instead of answering. A courage was rising that I had not felt in front of that beautiful woman. However, as soon as the door closed, it disappeared in a flash. Reflected in the golden elevator door was a sickly-looking man with a pale face, drooping shoulders, a frightened look, whom everyone seemed likely to laugh at if he ran about in the middle of Myeong-dong shouting 'Killer!' I tried to remember the last time I had gone out, but I couldn't. I looked up. A CCTV camera was attached to the ceiling. I smiled at the camera. It was really more of a twitch than a smile.

The elevator stopped, the door slid open and his 'private room' filled my gaze. The room could not help but fill my gaze. There was nothing in that space to block my view; it occupied the entire floor of the building, or judging by the height of the ceiling, two floors. The secretary had called it a 'private room' but if you were going to call it a room, my own room would have to be called something else, just a rathole or the palm of a hand, perhaps. Indeed, if this space fell into the category of room, the Olympic Gymnastics Arena would also have to be considered a kind of room.

There was a sofa in the middle of the room, a rocking chair by the window and a minibar in the corner. That was all. It was an empty space where people could play football. The entire new city could be seen at a glance through the large windows. It was the most dramatic way of expressing wealth. The most expensive thing in this country is space. Here, it was going to waste.

The Chairman was snoring quietly in the rocking chair. I coughed politely. In the empty space, my cough rang out louder than I expected. The snoring stopped. There was a moment of silence.

'Are you that guy?' The Chairman's voice was also louder than I expected, but when he stood up, I realised he was much shorter than he had looked on TV. In fact, many conquerors in history were short. Despite his short stature, he somehow felt overpowering. I didn't know what kind of guy he was talking about, but at such a moment the answer is always the same.

'Yes, sir.'

'Those things we asked for, you seem to have enjoyed dealing with them.'

I couldn't think of anything to say. I felt sweat breaking out on my fists, which were clenched tight with tension.

'Yes, thank you, sir. It's work, first of all … it's how I earn a living.' I coughed softly to clear my trembling voice.

He giggled. How many people must stutter in front of him? He walked slowly toward the minibar. The sound of his slippers dragging over the floor echoed in the empty room.

'These days, you know, no one knows how to work properly.'

'It's really the Company that does the work. I only do the planning …' My voice was shaking too much. That wasn't good, considering what was coming.

'Planning is important. When it comes to doing as they're told, I have tens of thousands of people under me. But so what? There's no one thinking. If you look closely, they're all just book-smart. What use is a diploma from a prestigious university in America? Because front and back are all blocked up, this won't do, that won't do. Pathetic.'

He clicked his tongue as he took out a glass from the minibar. Then, with a serious expression on his face, he held it up and examined it carefully before putting it down.

After taking a deep breath, I replied, barely managing to suppress my tremors, 'It's just a job, sir. I'm simply used to it.'

'Humble. Simply used to it … I like that.'

He took out a bottle of whiskey. As soon as I saw the bottle, I frowned spontaneously. The whiskey, known for its anti-forgery cap, was simply not up to snuff considering his position as Chairman. It might be a bit expensive when drinking it at a bar, but people like me wouldn't choose it if we were shopping at a large mart. The bottle of cheap whiskey and the wasted space didn't go together here. He opened it. I heard a snapping sound as the anti-forgery cap yielded. It reminded me of an advertisement I had seen in a men's magazine, which boasted that it was possible to refill a bottle with liquor by breaking the bottle's neck. He half-filled the glass but didn't add any ice. Then he carefully examined the glass for a moment, as if hoping to find an answer there.

'Would you like a drink, too?'

'I'm fine, sir.'

At that he smiled and nodded. Then he began to pour the remaining whiskey into the sink. As if admitting that it was not up to his level, he was pouring away all the remaining liquor that he had not yet drunk. Seeing that, I felt nervous. Some people might take it for a luxury, or an eccentricity of the rich, but because of my profession I had a good understanding of the lives of rich people. What it meant was all too clear to me.

'What goals do you have?'

He shook the glass. The amber whiskey swirled round.

'Sir?'

'Young people nowadays, they don't have any goals. Everyone had them in our times. When you were going to be a manager, when you were going to move, buy a house, how you were going to raise your children, things like that.'

I bowed my head for a moment. There had been times like that, it was true. That was possible in the seventies and eighties, until the 1997 IMF crisis, or when the president called for globalisation. Our fathers' lives had been epic. Because they had goals, failure or success was clear. But my friends didn't even know if they'd have a job in a year's time. Goals were something too grand for us.

'I don't think this is a world where there can be goals in life.'

'If you're a man, surely you should be full of nerve.'

'But life's not predictable. You don't know what's going to happen nowadays, even if you're in a company.'

Swallowing a sip of whiskey, the Chairman asked, 'A predictable life ... what if you could live that kind of life in our company? I'll give you three, or five times the amount you get now.'

I closed my eyes tightly. I imagined the sum. I sighed. I replied, trying as hard as I could not to show my feelings, 'Fantastic.'

I wasn't surprised, because I had been expecting his offer. But I hadn't thought about what kind of expression I should adopt when I heard the suggestion, so I just looked non-committal.

He went on. 'It won't be too bad. You won't have to kill people. I just need you to take care of my personal safety. You'll get a title, you'll get a business card, you'll get an office for yourself, and as for your position … what about chief of staff?'

I smiled instead of answering. Chief of staff in the head-quarters of a large company, at my age! It would be an unprecedented promotion. All my peers from college were still just assistant managers. At my age, being chief of staff was a luxury that could normally only be enjoyed by the immediate family of the Chairman. The pay wasn't bad, either, and best of all, I wouldn't have to kill people. It was quite an attractive proposition. There was no reason to refuse.

'Other than that,' he continued, 'there will be a moderate number of benefits. Let's start with getting the car and the house set up.'

My smile widened. It was a wonderful thing to imagine.

'By the way, you'll have to get yourself some suits made to wear to work. And you should have a congratulatory drink with your friends.'

He held out a card. It wasn't just an ordinary credit card. It was a card that only a handful of people in the whole world have. There had been an article in the men's magazine where I saw that whiskey ad, about an Arab millionaire who had applied for the card in question and been rejected. The title of the article was '10 Things the Super-Rich Enjoy'. In the article, there was a list of the items that the best people should have. Among the items listed, that credit card was placed between a private plane and a yacht with large sails.

Considering the reports about the Chairman's eccentric personality, which sounded like mere rumours, given our relationship and the location, his attitude could almost be called unconventional. By all accounts, there was no reason to refuse. Except for one thing.

'It's not something I can resolve on my own. As you know, I belong to the Company.' It was unwise to say no to the Chairman. Knowing this, my voice was bound to tremble.

At that he emptied his glass in one gulp and in a rather exasperated voice, asked, 'You think the Company can protect you, but how do you suppose I know who you are?'

He was right. If it was a reliable kind of operation, only the Company should have had information about me. Of course, this was a question that I had been expecting. Nevertheless, I could no longer hide the fact that I was trembling; I was much better at hiding behind a keyboard and monitor. I wouldn't be able to hold on much longer if we talked too long. I slowly started pacing around the large space that I was reluctant to call a room.

'If you don't mind, sir, may I ask how you figured it out?'

He put down the glass, beaming. 'I'm a businessman. I made a deal. "If you don't let me meet him," I told them, "I won't give you any more work."'

'So the Company succumbed to pressure. Maybe I'm not the one you're looking for after all.'

'You don't have to worry about that. We've already checked.'

He followed my pacing figure with his eyes, fiddling with the glass on the minibar as he did so.

'Think about it,' he said. 'Do you think that the Company didn't know I would make this offer when they introduced you to me? They knew. Even if you accept my offer, what you're worried about won't happen.'

I paced by the rocking chair, listening to his words. He seemed to be trying to persuade me. The night view of the new city unfolded before my eyes. I could see buildings and apartment complexes built by his company in the distance. Here he was looking down at his possessions, his kingdom. This seat was his throne. I turned around and looked up for a moment. Just above my head, I noticed a dusty-looking vent. Dry hot air was flowing out of the vent, yet still I was feeling cold and shivering. Or rather, I was so nervous that my whole body was shaking. I turned to him, then said with a wry smile, 'Surely, sir, you know that for the Company to betray my trust is a completely different matter from me betraying its trust.'

His expression changed. Rumour had it that the two things he hated most were being refused and not being in possession of something. I'd heard that it was his personality that had created the large company he now controlled. It was dangerous to go against the Company, but it didn't seem wise to offend the Chairman when I was right in front of him, either.

'Let me check what the Company's intentions are,' I said. 'And if there's no problem, I'll accept your offer.'

I turned and looked at the card on the minibar. The card, one of the ten things the super-rich enjoy, sparkled in the light. His expression turned gentle again. Cold sweat ran down my back.

With a victorious smile, he held out a hand. I rubbed my sweaty palms against my vest and held out mine. We shook hands. His hands were smaller and softer than I had anticipated.

'But have you figured out who's behind that?'

His expression flinched as he let go of my hand. I pointed to the empty bottle of whiskey he had put down.

'That's too cheap for you.'

At that he burst into laughter. It was a cheerful laugh, but I didn't laugh along with him. I didn't need to curry favour, I wasn't a member of his staff yet. So his laughter faded into a rather lonesome echo. It is so obvious when a man is in a situation where he can only drink whiskey from a newly opened bottle with the latest anti-forgery cap for fear of being poisoned.

'It's not that there's no one for me to suspect. But there are so many people like that. It's what business is all about.'

He spoke boldly, but for a moment, a lonely look flashed across his face. I nodded. He seemed so seedy, all alone in this enormous room. I boarded the elevator. While the door was closing, I looked at him one last time. He was sitting in his rocking chair as when I arrived, but there was no feeling of surprise or pressure like before. He was at the apex of a pyramid comprised of tens of thousands of people, but he could not escape from one floor of this building. The room was very big, but no matter how big it was, it was only a prison. No matter how big the pyramid was, it was just a tomb, nothing more. No matter what the legends said, in my eyes he was just an old man with the title of Chairman, frightened and bluffing. The elevator door closed and the Chairman was left alone. I came out into the world, and returned home in the black saloon that the owner could no longer ride out of fear.

At the same time, I completed the task that the Company had given me. I had told the Chairman that I would inform him of the Company's response, but I didn't need to. Before I could call him back, the Chairman had to be hospitalised.

A few days after I left the room, he caught pneumonia. While being treated after being hospitalised, the pneumonia turned into sepsis and various complications developed at the same time. Within a week, he was reduced to not being able to go to the bathroom without a wheelchair, and a few days later, he no longer had to go to the bathroom as a tube was inserted in his urethra and he was equipped with nappies. And he never saw the following season.

Thus died one of the Company's biggest clients. But it didn't affect the Company much because they had a new client. The new client was the Chairman's son. The Chairman's cause of death was given as sepsis but I prefer to say that it was restructuring.

The Company never betrayed me. After his son's clumsy attempt at poisoning him failed, the frightened Chairman had locked himself in his 'very private room'. Later, the son was looking for an expert and asked the Company to help, but there was a lack of detailed information. In order to prepare a plan, I had to see the space where the attempt was to be made, so I went there myself. No one had ever been in his private room except himself.

What is needed for the natural death of a customer is foresight. We need to know exactly what the customer will do in the future. Foresight is not an ability. There may be a super-human being with that ability, but I work through thorough analysis. That's why I need so much information. And the most important thing I have to analyse through that information is the customer's desires. We act according to our desires. Nothing happens by chance, not even the smallest decisions that we are oblivious to. For example, the pastor in the second novel I wrote was caught in a conflict between a desire for fame and sexual fulfilment. It was probably a distorted desire for power that was expressed in the form of adultery. God's shepherd, infidelity, a meticulous person-ality, a high reputation, his doctor ... all this showed what desires he had, what contradictions he battled. It was not difficult to predict the choices he would make at the point where these might collide. When his desire for fame was in crisis, he was very likely to cling to a very small hope, even if it was fanciful and false. If the desire for fame intervened to suggest that he could control the situation, the choice soon became inevitable. That's how the air conditioner came crashing down.

The same was true of the Chairman. The view he was looking at from his window was not merely a view. His kingdom was in crisis and the rocking chair had to be in the right place to maintain his belief that he was in control. A paranoid obsession with his own safety, a firm desire to rule over his kingdom: those factors limited his actions. So I could plan without a shadow of doubt. The location was perfect for pouring an aerosol of cultivated pneumococcus through the air vent.

Once I was out of his 'private room' it was so simple. In older people, pneumonia easily develops into sepsis, and antibiotics do not work well on sepsis. Of course he might have recovered. However, the Chairman was never given any genuine antibiotics. So another natural death was created for the client.

The client didn't have much time. The son, who was in a hurry, made a very good offer to the Company, and the Company made a much better offer to me. The fact that the Chairman had found me was also part of the plan. Each person had simply acted in their own best interest, that was all. To repeat what I said, structure is the only thing that survives restructuring. There are no exceptions. No one is ever free.

Q & A

At this point, I want to talk about some of the things that readers might be really curious about. The most common question ordinary people have about this job is how much I earn. That is actually everyone's most general question about every job, perhaps because, after all, the most important standard of value that everyone can relate to is money.

The money I earn is similar to the annual salary of a lawyer. To be exact, the pay for killing three people in a year is a little lower than for the average lawyer; for killing four it is a little higher. The money increases exponentially with the difficulty of the work. In the case of the Chairman, I pocketed fifteen times my daily pay, including special travel expenses and risk allowances. But I've rarely had more than five deaths a year. Natural death requires quite a lot of preparation and it's hard for the Company.

That doesn't mean that I am busy. Even in the year when I killed five people, I think I actually worked for less than half the year. The rest of the time, I had six months without work. That might seem like a very good job. But that is only the time spent planning a murder. I spend most of the rest of my time preparing for the next task. At best, it's impossible to understand just what I'm preparing for. So many people dream of a perfect crime, but they almost always fail because they are not thoroughly prepared. My enemies are detectives, coroners and scientists on the ground. They look for criminals with invisible evidence, while I transform the meaning of the visible evidence into something different. They are smart, have high-tech equipment and have mastered scientific theory. Maybe everyone is smarter than me.

The only strategic advantage I have is that I know who they are and how they work, but they don't know who I am or how I work. So the moment those positions are reversed, I shall have no choice but to lose this game. And even a single failure, a tiny mistake, would be fatal. Therefore, I have to adapt myself fully and perfectly to the system. I train myself to operate without error as part of the system.

When I wake up in the morning, I go to an online newsgroup where forensic scientists from around the world exchange papers and check submissions that came in during the night. Imagine, all written only in English, and rife with jargon. One of the happiest things about choosing to do this job was that I no longer had to study TOEIC, but the first thing I did when I started researching data was to buy a new electronic dictionary. Sadly, there were no Korean texts anywhere. It was easy to get the data itself because I had the internet, but I had to virtually study abroad to do it.

Newsgroups that exchange views and share papers among scholars were my saviours. Of course, that is only how I feel now; at first, the whole thing left a really bad taste in my mouth. It took me all day just to read the list of newly published papers and a summary of their contents. I complained to my Manager every day, asking her to let me attend forensic seminars, assign me a professional translator, hire a consultant or steal data from the National Forensic Service.

It took three months for the Company to respond. That's why mine is only a camouflage company. And indeed I did receive internal data from the National Forensic Service. It was all a bit crazy. I became more afraid of the Company. There was no end to how far their arms could reach.

Anyway, now it's enough for me to look at the newsgroups for an hour or two. The trick is similar to going to porn sites and choosing pornographic videos. The reaction is clear soon after both are uploaded. Whether it's enthusiastic support, surprise or even disgust, something bites people. Those are the first things to be identified. Of course I'm not a forensic scientist, so my judgement doesn't exactly match their reactions. I don't want to learn how to catch criminals, I want to know how to avoid being caught. I sort out some of the things I think are essential or important and send them to the camouflage company on my business card. Then they translate it. It usually takes a day or two at most. It's hard to read the translations, too, but I'm not in a position to distinguish between cold and hot rice.

By the way, thanks to this system, I am more up to date on forensic science than anyone else in our country. Information is the best weapon to help survive in an endgame.

After the paper search, I spend the morning doing general research. There is no limit here. There are no exceptions, from pharmacology to chemistry, psychology, engineering, even statistics. To create a database for murder, this information is organised systematically on my computer. Unlike forensic science, it sets out general and solid theories.

Because we don't know when and what we might need. This is something I haven't told the Company – but they might already know: the types of natural deaths I plan should be more or less consistent with people's average cause of death. It may seem a little obsessive, but this is very important for a natural death. This is because a death which deviates greatly from the average statistical cause of death is a big potential clue.

The most competent serial killers are doctors and nurses. They are taking over the title for serial killers who have killed the most people. They naturally have access to victims, are well versed in medical knowledge and can easily get their hands on all kinds of drugs. In addition, they have good enough minds, equipment and environments to dream up perfect crimes. In terms of circumstances, they are blessed murderers who surpass me. But the fact that they have the top title among serial killers means that even they are eventually caught.

It is the statistics that explain how they are caught. Pass the data on mortality rates in each hospital to a competent statistician and they will find any unnatural deaths there. Death is an indicator of something gone wrong, even if at first glance it doesn't seem to make much difference.

Suppose a nurse gets a job at a hospital and four more patients die of unprovoked heart attacks that year than the year before. The nurse is a self-confident serial killer who kills only four people a year. There seems to be little chance of her being caught. But heart attacks don't happen in hospitals as often as people think they do. Frequent seizures occur, so then people undergo surgery and die during surgery, but very few die from a single heart attack – because in a hospital a lot of people can come running right away and revive the cardiopulmonary system. Many of the direct causes of death from heart disease are actually because of the side effects of a weakened heart. If eight people died each year from heart attacks at the hospital until last year, her appearance would have increased heart attack deaths by fifty per cent. Now, that's going to smell a bit fishy. They will immediately find hospital records from her previous job and compare the number of heart attack deaths before and after she worked there.

Let me give you another example. Suppose a psychopathic doctor kills one in ten people each time he operates, pretending they died during surgery. It might not seem like much. The people at the hospital may also think of him simply as an unlucky doctor. But statistics will show that his misfortune leads to far higher mortality rates than other doctors. Because even though one in ten may not seem that many, the resulting number of deaths is statistically higher. And as the statistics accumulate, more information about a human being is revealed.

We tend to believe that we are exceptional beings, set apart from statistics. But no human being is unique. If enough statistical information is accumulated, even tastes that you do not recognise as your own will be revealed. How do you select your victims? It is profiling that pushes this to the extreme. If an act is repeated, it becomes even more difficult to hide it statistically with even the smallest clue. There is no room for escape if psychological analysis is involved. Given enough data and time, statisticians can approximate the number of patients a serial killer has killed and identify the culprit. Creating a natural death is by no means easy. For that, you have to cheat on chance and probability.

After lunch, the papers I requested the previous day arrive in translation. I read them, organise what I need and enter that into the database. Most of the data is not needed right away. Not all high-tech theories apply directly to the field, and there are some hypotheses and concepts that have been controversial for quite some time. Also, hard-working law enforcers don't really know as much about cutting-edge theories as I do. Even if they do, it is up to officials to introduce the related equipment. Budgeting for those things takes a number of bureaucratic steps and only happens much later. Perhaps it will be five years at the earliest and ten years at the latest when the papers I am reading will begin to have meaning in the field. Therefore, it is a matter of investing for the future rather than using everything straight away. For a database to exert force in a system, the amount of information accumulated is vital. I need only to look through the National Forensic Service's list and I can see at once what to put in and what to leave out, what to use and what not to use. Such is the power of the database. Of course, before that, the police in charge of the crime scene will have dealt with the incident, so they won't have to investigate it again.

If you're in law enforcement or a man devoted to justice, every word I say will sound terrible. But there's nothing for you to worry about, nothing to be angry about. Few people take the same path as me. In most cases, they bribe prosecutors, hire a former judge-turned-lawyer or just go to jail. Some people may produce false medical certificates or complain of mental illness. The bottom line is that there are countless people you can't arrest, without worrying about me. As I said earlier, no matter how many times I kill in a year, it will be hard to get past five. That number is less than a quarter of the daily traffic fatalities. Just catching drunk drivers and cracking down on the use of mobile phones while driving would save far more lives. That is the reality that statistics tell us.

After spending the day like this, I eat dinner and watch TV alone, mainly American detective dramas such as *CSI*, *Numbers* and *Without a Trace*. That kind of thing doesn't really help much. The equipment used is over the top, and the actual collection of evidence or criminal proof is not that simple. In reality, if you only had to put a sample in a large machine and spin it around to be able to analyse anything, and if the screen on a CCTV system could be expanded indefinitely in high definition, then criminal activities would probably be completely unprofitable. In addition, in such fictional dramas, the criminals are almost always caught. It's hardly a learning experience.

But investigators can understand human logic. At least their characters are rooted in reality. Understanding their logic provides an idea of how to get round it. I keep track of their ideas without fail. After all, I only spend my days preparing to kill someone naturally.

There is nothing to envy in the fact that a year of my work only occupies half the year. Of course, no one is imposing this arrangement on me. But I don't want to fail. Even if I fail, my chances of going to jail or coming up against the police are close to zero. I'm more afraid of the Company. Restructuring in the place where I work is really scary. Therefore, I set up an optimised daily framework to create natural deaths and settle down inside it.

My only leisure activity in this dry life is collecting old DVDs and watching the documentary channel that I switch to when I'm alone. What I enjoy watching most is *Animal Kingdom*. The last time I cried was when I was watching an episode about a male mountain gorilla's life. His was a whole life full of drama. According to *Animal Kingdom*, drama can be defined in four ways: birth, fighting, mating, death. These things are essentially epic.

* * *

I feel sorry for the people who are reading this. I'm not a funny killer. After spending all day sitting at your own company's desk, you don't want to hear the story of a killer who sits at his computer eight hours a day. Maybe the people who carry out my plans have a more dramatic life than I do. But basically, I don't plan for high-risk situations. Putting them in danger is no different from putting myself in danger. In most cases, what the implementers of my plans do is simply move, change, remove or return something behind other people's backs. Our victims die when a few of these unfortunate coincidences overlap in succession. Believe it or not, that's all. Modern life is repeated every week, every month, every year. Therefore, even the slightest crack in the axis that supports the repetition is fatal. Anyway, I'm sure the implementers of my plans have as little fun as I do. Modern society is a divided society, and everyone has a similarly dull life. Even killers.

My week is like this. It's always the same, even if you mix up a few days. The only things that make me feel the flow of time are Sundays, which come once a week, and Wednesdays, when I go into the office. Yes, even killers go into the office. Going into the office at the company named on my business card, I'm supposed to telecommute in New York time. The people at the office think that I am reporting the work of the Korean branch to the headquarters, receiving and delivering instructions and giving appropriate advice on the Korean market. I'd love to meet the genius who made up this excuse. Thanks to it, I am not only able to entrust to them miscellaneous tasks such as translating papers or collecting materials, but I also remain faithful to the title on my business card. So everyone in the office knows me, and some even pretend to be close.

When I get to work, I sit alone in my office and do things that are not that different from what I do at home. We have an office get-together around the end of the year. That's how I become a white-collar worker. Forget about the killer in the movie who crosses the world with beautiful women, intrigues and colourful action. As far as I know, there are at least three kinds of killers in the reality of Korea.

One is an ambitious gang member. Wanting to grow up in an organisation and prove their existence with cruelty, they find their role models in movies. That's how they earn their stars. The stars are medals, pride and rank to them. If they prove their worth, they get a heavy sentence and grow old in prison. And by the time they get out, everything has changed. The organisations have changed, people have changed and rules have changed. Junior players who are as ambitious and cruel as they used to be are after their backs. Somehow, they're similar to office workers who are given early retirement. It's probably a long time after they've been treated as scumbags and been made to resign that they realise it's not the passionate and cruel but the strategic and business-like person who survives in this tournament. Or maybe they never realise it.

The most common illusion about organised crime is to think that it is something marked by violence and power. Actually, the gangs are basically similar to McDonald's. A number of irregular workers and franchise branches are the essence of the organisation. The main difference is that instead of hamburgers, they sell violence and fear.

But violence beyond demand only increases the risk of the business. Excessive violence attracts the attention of the media and police. It is similar to the way companies that overproduce cannot handle surplus inventory and so collapse easily. Ultimately, the killer in an organisation is always a pawn unless he is very competent. The highest point they can reach is just high enough to allow new young people to hope and dream, devoting themselves to the organisation without knowing anything. With the stars they earn, they become the envy of their subordinates and are respected within the organisation, but they are destined to be used and then abandoned when things eventually go wrong, as if there were only so many fantasies allowed to blue-collar people. Pawns are nothing but pawns, and it's people elsewhere who lead the game. Even the organisation is ultimately nothing more than the pawn of other people.

Another type of killer is the day labourer hired temporarily by errand centres, also known as troubleshooters. Most of them are people who are prepared to do anything for money. Examples of this kind are endless, ranging from loan-ridden farmers, gamblers who have squandered their assets, trafficked ethnic Koreans and day labourers who need money because someone in their family is sick. The bottom line is, their criminal records are clean, they are poor and desperate fools who are even willing to sell their organs at that minute for money.

They take advantage of what they call a blind spot in the way investigations are carried out. When the police try to determine how someone has been killed, they first investigate ex-convicts who have criminal records similar to those involved. Therefore, it is unlikely that the day labourers will be suspected. If they leave no evidence or fingerprints on the scene, if the police take the wrong direction in the initial investigation, they sometimes succeed. But they're new and they're killing for the first time. Sometimes the murder itself fails, and more often than not they do leave traces of their crime. Of course there are people who succeed; they make up a large part of the unsolved cases. After all, investigations are somewhat manualised and although they are termed scientific investigations, they still have to rely on old-fashioned processes like fingerprints. To be honest, it would be hard to find a criminal who has left no fingerprints and had no interaction with the victim, even if Sherlock Holmes came back to life. The problem is that not being caught isn't the end. Such killers are always disposable.

For two reasons. Suppose they left some hair or blood at the scene that could be tested for the killer's genes. And if they unfortunately leave the same hair at the next murder scene, the police will know that the two crimes were committed by the same criminal. Then, of course, they look for links between the two cases. That includes the possibility of contractual killings. It's only a matter of time before the police start to notice that a certain crime is a hit-and-run murder. It is easy for anyone to infer that the person who benefits the most from the victim's death must have made the request. If they get a warrant and track bank accounts, they will find a suspicious transfer of funds. Now, take the suspect to the interrogation room, push and pull him about, and in all likelihood he will start to talk. Therefore, the level of risk is completely different when ordering a second murder just because the first one was successful.

The second reason is sadder. Murderers are usually ordinary people who have lived good lives. Above all, the premise that their criminal record should be clean proves that clearly. Imagine a good man who has never been embroiled in a drunk-driving or assault case killing some-one one day for money.

They're ruined.

There are various ways. Alcohol, drug addiction, homelessness, going crazy, in severe cases suicide. Killing someone leaves an irreversible scar on a person's soul. Eventually they are all ruined in some way. Some of them look fine. But even they only *look* fine. The reason I know this so well is because I have restructured one such person.

He was a poor, simple-looking young man in his twen-ties who couldn't possibly be a headache for anyone and was desperate for some money. It was a very interesting case, so I asked the Manager about the situation. I didn't expect she'd tell me much because previously she had never told me anything, even if I asked. However, on this occasion, she answered candidly. Perhaps she enjoyed that the Company was being commissioned by a competitor. It was the errand centre that had commissioned the killing. It had been commissioned by a company where the main business was contracting.

A year before, the man had killed a woman around his age at the request of an errand centre because he needed the money for his younger brother, who was suffering from heart disease. The woman, who was an inveterate marriage fraudster, was so attractive that anyone would fall in love with her at first sight. Once promises turned into decep-tion, love turned into hatred, then someone paid money because of the hatred, and the young man received the money. The woman died, and the work was very well done. The body was brutally mutilated. The hate-filled customer was satisfied, the police determined it was a grudge crime and investigated it, but all the suspects had alibis. It was a very rare, tidy job for a good young man with no criminal record. So the satisfied errand centre was willing to pay.

But the errand centre didn't think he'd be fine for long, because there was no one who looked fine after such a brutal murder who didn't break down a few months later. The younger brother had surgery and was doing well. If things had stopped there, it would have been a generally satisfactory ending.

But it was only the beginning. Soon after, when the young man came back to the errand centre looking subdued, everyone at the centre was surprised. He was still just the same as when he received the money. With a calm, smiling look, he asked if they had any more work for him. The centre, reluctant to give him another murder for the reasons mentioned earlier, asked if he would like a delivery job. Compared to murder, it was simple and it seemed okay to trust him with such work if he was still sane after killing someone. From the young man's point of view, too, it would be much safer and better paid. But surprisingly, the young man refused. When asked if he needed money, the young man briefly answered 'No' and disappeared.

Half a year later, the errand centre began to hear strange rumours through a contact they had planted in the police. Information suggested that a series of murders were taking place in a satellite city of Seoul in Gyeonggi-do, where mainly young people lived. However, the method employed was exactly the same as the way in which the young man had killed the woman who was the marriage fraudster. These were all young women, with mutilated bodies. The errand centre did its utmost to obtain the list of victims, which was being kept secret and not made known to the media by any means. When they looked at the list, there was no need to think twice. The police had already narrowed down the investigation to the point where they speculated that the criminal must be living in the same neighbourhood as the young man. So they turned to us. It was necessary to kill the young man naturally without attracting the attention of the police.

I was very happy to arrange for him to have an accident. The scaffolding broke at the construction site where he was working. He fell from the twenty-first floor. It just so happened that there was no safety net, and by 'accident', he hadn't attached a safety belt. The reason why the errand centre commissioned us was simple but clear. The fourth name on the list of victims was none other than the young man's younger sister. The incident remained unclassified. And the serial killings also became dead to the world in a police station filing cabinet, still unknown to the media.

The luckiest among the second class of killers are those who make some kind of mistake and so fail to kill their target or get arrested. In any case, they are used and then abandoned. Failure is their last chance to go on living a human life. As Nietzsche warned, once you enter the abyss, there's no way of getting out again without becoming a monster.

Finally, there are people like me who belong to the Company. I have no idea whether they all belong to the same Company as me, nor how many there are besides me. Maybe I'm the only one, but it's highly unlikely. But if there's more of us, it could be your friend, your neighbour, or the person sitting next to you right now. In short, people no different from other white-collar workers. Until not so long ago I thought we were different. And I believed that there must be a very small number of us. After all, it's a matter of killing people. But now I can speak with confidence. We are just plain white collar and middle class. And there are a lot more of us than you might imagine. Naturally it's not like in the movies. Repetition, routine, division of labour and efficiency. Unlike pre-modern, primitive, pawn-like gang killers and non-regular killers who are either disposable or abandoned in a capitalist society, we are able to survive because we have adapted to capitalist society and are part of the system.

Anyway, I reckon that's all the things you'll be wondering about in my boring job.

Business Relationships

In the office, I am usually considered a good co-worker. The biggest reason is that I have no direct conflicts with anyone and ask no favours. What's strange about working life is that the less contact you have with people, the better the impression you make on others. Unlike them, I was officially a member of staff dispatched from headquarters, although it was a bit ironic that the headquarters did not actually exist. Once, the question of why I had been dispatched by the head office at such a young age was a hot topic in the office. If anyone had asked, I would have told them the truth. I'd accidentally applied for an internship when I was in college, and passed. Of course no one asked. There were no personnel files about me, so I suppose I'd been the subject of merry gossip for quite a while.

They decided to make me an MBA graduate from a prestigious American university. There was a lot of talk about East Coast, West Coast, Ivy League or not, but finally I somehow became a 'mother's friend's son', which even I could admire. A 'mother's friend's son' whose existence was as ambiguous as Batman or Superman, who was good at studying, full of filial piety, handsome and good at making money, as well as well mannered. I long to show them my report card proving that I had to take all the vacation courses to make up my credits. But I haven't tried to correct the rumours. It's true that I was having a bit of fun, but in fact, few people were that close to me. There was one person, actually, who I met privately – I'll tell you more about that later – but to explain that relationship, it was only closer in the way a star 50,000 light years away is closer than one 100,000 light years away. After all, both are big distances. I wasn't particularly cold, but I made my co-workers feel uncomfortable, and I had no reason to approach them either. Besides, I had so many secrets to keep.

The only person in the office who really knew what my job was was the branch manager. Or rather, strictly speaking, he knew that I belonged to the Company and did something scary. What that was exactly I left entirely up to his imagination. Once a week, I stopped by his room for a formal report before leaving work. Of course, I was on the receiving end, and he did the reporting. Each time he showed an incredibly servile attitude. He treated me with deference, although I was his nephew's age, and he always insisted he was comfortable with that, but he did not treat anyone in the office except me in that way. He was the kind of person who pretended to be somewhat friendly in order to hide the fact that he was uncomfortable with me, but that made the relationship even more uncomfortable.

Once, after an office supper, we went on to a karaoke bar. A new employee had arrived that day, and we were welcoming him. The branch manager tagged along for the second round, and everyone was hinting to him that he should go home. On the way to the bar, the other employees constantly urged him to leave, saying, 'Won't your wife be worried?' and

'You seem to have been overdoing things today.' But he was adamant. Maybe he followed along because I hadn't gone home. He kept watching me. Any other time, I would have gone home early, too. But that day, everyone was holding on to me, saying they wanted to see me drunk. I didn't want to spoil the fun, so I was intending to sit down with them for a while, then sneak away, using a visit to the toilet as an excuse. Fortunately, I had a good head for drink, but there was no telling what I might say when I was really drunk. Anyway, once we were at the bar, since it was a welcoming party for the new employee, he naturally grabbed the microphone for the first song. Just as he was beginning, the branch manager, who had gone to the toilet, came in.

He shouted angrily at the new employee in a slurred voice, 'Why are you being so tactless? It's been ages since we've had such an important person with us!'

Then he snatched the mic. The new employee looked helpless, thinking he must have made a really big mistake. The branch manager squeezed past the knees of the other employees, holding on to the microphone until he reached where I was sitting, right on the inside.

'Here you are, sing away.'

A lot of thoughts came to my mind and disappeared in a flash, from *Is this guy trying to screw me over?* to *Is he crazy?* Along with them came and went feelings that were complicated to explain, but in the end, what remained was pity. He belonged to a generation that had survived in this way. Just as the muscles of his body had degenerated with time and fat accumulated on his stomach, his senses were decrepit. He was too old to curry someone's favour now. I looked at the microphone in front of me. I thought about singing in an atmosphere so awkward it seemed like the end of the party. I didn't like the idea.

I led him outside, put him in a taxi and sent him home. He still hadn't got the feel of things and shouted, 'Oh, I'm sorry, you don't have to do this!'

After he left, I stood at the side of the road and smoked a cigarette. Then I went home. Fortunately, I wouldn't have to see him until the following week. Because I didn't want to see him the next morning hovering awkwardly over my desk, asking whether he had made a mistake.

Thanks to the branch manager, the people in the office seem to believe the idle rumour that I have an MBA. When I see him, I wonder how he sees me. Of course, the person receiving the Company's instructions must be higher up on the food chain, but I always wondered how such a timid person got involved in the Company in the first place. The answer came about four years after I started working with him.

It was probably the week before the Chuseok holiday, near the end of September. We were supposed to have a party at the office that day, and I was trying to back out again under the guise of working on New York local time. There's no Chuseok in New York. I wanted to tell him that he was the reason why I wanted to back out, but if I said that, he would spend the whole holiday wondering what I meant.

'Well, you see, sometimes attending office parties demands a natural relationship with the other employees and ...'

'Is that an order?'

'Oh, no, no. Well, well, I'm just ...'

His forehead was covered with beads of sweat. He was a man with whom jokes really didn't work. Or maybe ours was a relationship where a sense of humour didn't work.

'Don't worry. It's not like I'm going to eat you.' I stood up smiling.

He too stood up, with a smile on his face that was more like a grimace.

'Then just think carefully.'

'Yes, see you next week …'

It was an incredibly awkward moment. As I headed for the door, I could hear him swallowing hard. To break this awkward moment, I said what I thought was the most normal thing.

'By the way, how's your family?'

At that, his legs began to tremble like an aspen. He looked as if he had peed in his pants.

'Oh, I know, I was impertinent … Please, forgive me.'

Suddenly he fell to his knees with his hands on the floor and stayed like that without looking up. Thanks to his position, I could see his trembling buttocks. Fortunately, he had his head down, or the look on my face would have really been worth seeing. I told him to get up. Frightened, he was on the verge of tears as he clumsily began to make a long excuse. I didn't want to hear any more. I just left the room. There were two possibilities. He might have had someone in his family killed by the Company. Or maybe the Company was holding his family hostage and threatening them. Indeed, what head of a household is not held hostage by the demands of earning his family's livelihood? The important thing was that he was just as much a slave to the Company as I was. I didn't feel sorry for him. No, it was more that he looked ugly. I could have explained my situation to him. Then we might have comforted each other. But I didn't. Because I am comfortable with my side of things.

As I left the office, the woman in charge of bookkeeping smiled at me.

Her smile banished my unpleasant feelings a little. She was answering the phone at that moment and with one hand made a sign to indicate that she would call me later.

Although they had changed several times, the woman in charge of bookkeeping around then was the only person in the office who showed direct good will toward me. Maybe it was because she knew my salary was higher than that of anyone else in the office. She knew just what a good thing money was. She hated her name, Hyeon-gyeong. I once asked why.

She replied, 'Do you know how many people come up when I search for my name on social network services like Cyworld?'

She was like a front runner of the consumerist craze that had just started to spread. Great American dramas had begun to spread illusions about working women on cable TV, and fantasies about something incomprehensible called 'cool' were everywhere, there was no avoiding them. Still in her early twenties, she loved luxury goods, and fashion and luxury goods were a kind of standard that distinguished her from others with the same name. I don't know if it's because I only went to the office once a week, but I'd never seen her wearing the same shoes twice. But the handbag was always the same. I hope you don't misunderstand me. It's not that I found her disgusting or disliked her. Besides, I don't think I'm in a position to judge. After all, it's surely a hundred times better to love luxury goods than to kill people. I liked Hyeon-gyeong because she didn't talk about love or trust. Those are really useless words.

At least once a year, plans had to be made to restructure spouses for reasons of insurance and inheritance. You think they didn't talk about love or trust while they were dating and when they got married? Even if it's not certain, a clever person would surely have talked about such things right up to the moment he had her killed. Indeed, he might have found scraps of love left while he was weeping in a funeral home after she died. Of course, love can cool off. They might change their minds or break up. I'm not saying we should deny that. The law has a system of divorce in place to prepare for such circumstances. But they did not opt for that. Instead, with the very lips that said they loved her, they contacted the Company and checked that a natural death was really possible.

I once killed the spouse of a very famous man. A month later, I had to watch him on a morning television show crying and going on about how much he had loved his wife. It was no different between other men and women. Maybe they had really loved one another. That made it all the more terrible. So I much preferred women who were honest with their desires because they were gold diggers or sex workers. Of course, I had other, greater reasons for liking such women.

Hyeon-gyeong called me often. I'm not someone who goes in for affectionate chats on the phone, I like to cut things short after talking briefly. Nevertheless, she kept calling me, asking questions such as, 'Have you eaten?' or 'What are you doing today?' Of course I was not stupid enough to think that she called because she was really curious if I had eaten. Just because she loved fantasy so much, I wanted to help her believe that I was really hooked.

It was almost four months after she started calling that Hyeon-gyeong and I went out for a meal together. I thought she'd stop calling earlier, but she was quite insistent. We went to a restaurant which often figured in magazines and on the internet, with a famous standard dating menu. People like those you see in movies sat in an interior that seemed cut out of a magazine, eating the kind of food photographed in cookbooks, as if they were living proof that life is really like that. I once read in a book that 'the purpose of art lies in deluding people into thinking that life is something worth living.' If this was right, this kind of specious appearance is the art that supports our lives. I thought I could see why women loved this kind of plausibility. For this kind of plausible reason, we also sat down and ordered food with long foreign-sounding names that twisted our tongues with their unknown pronunciation and meaning. The various methods of killing someone was a perfect subject to discuss in front of a rare steak from which red juice seeped out every time I cut into it, but it was not something I wanted to brag about to anyone. However, weekend soap operas that I did not even watch, or ways of calculating accounts using Excel, could hardly be considered a hot topic of conversation either. The professional way she counted money was pretty sexy but it was too early to bring that up as a talking point. The atmosphere was more awkward than I had expected and we were asking each other useless questions hoping to find something that would stick. As we were running out of topics, I had no choice but to bring up what I knew about her. The only thing I knew about Hyeon-gyeong was that she always carried the same bag.

'Is there a special story attached to your bag?'

'What?'

'You never change it, while your clothes and shoes change.'

'Wow, you've been watching. I thought you weren't interested in me.'

'The red high heels went really well with that bag.'

'Really, I'll have to wear them again next time.'

'The bag is always the same anyway.'

'Well, it's not really. I just like this brand ...'

'I don't know, but I think Louis Vuitton is quite expensive. Does our company pay you that well?'

'No way, the work's leisurely and we can go home early, but the pay's a bit stingy. Where I worked before, it used to be overtime, extra work, every day, until I got so fed up that I moved.'

'I see. I don't go to work in the office very often ... and I'm not even part of the Korean branch.'

'Don't you get bored working alone at home?'

'No, honestly, it suits me fine. There's no one whose voice I can't stand, and there's no one I have to keep an eye on.'

'But aren't you lonely sometimes?'

'Well, I'm used to it.'

I shrugged my shoulders. There was an awkward silence for a moment. I realised it was not the answer she wanted to hear. I was on the wrong track. But it couldn't be helped. It was clear why Hyeon-gyeong was interested in me, so I needed to look vaguely stupid. In that respect, the mistake would certainly work to my advantage. She started to pick up the pieces skilfully.

'Anyway, I got this as a gift.' She lifted her bag slightly as she spoke.

'Oh, so that's why you always carry it with you. I guess you got it from someone very special?'

'No, I like it because it's by LV. I really like their designs and image. Why, to be perfectly honest, if someone bought me a new tote bag by them, I'd probably fall in love with the guy.' She smiled, pointing to the brand's metal initials embedded in the bag.

Love ... I turned my head and looked out of the window for a moment. I had all the information I needed. When should I make a date? In the meantime, our dessert arrived.

She asked, 'What do you usually do on Sundays?'

'I watch *Animal Kingdom*. It's quite fun.'

'Wow, you must like animals. I have a puppy.'

I smiled bitterly.

'Well, perhaps it would be more accurate to say that you like *Animal Kingdom* rather than animals.'

'I do have a favourite animal, though. Gorillas.'

'Then shall we go to the zoo next time?'

Hyeon-gyeong smiled. I wondered to myself whether there was a good place to stay near the zoo. I'd look it up on the internet once I got back home.

So our second date was at the zoo. The zoo itself was incredibly dreary. The animals there somehow looked like people. They all hung around in their cages with the kind of anxious expressions that could otherwise only be seen on the bus going to work. Except for the animals that were asleep. Because most animals are actually nocturnal. Were they happier by night than they were now? Anyway, we went to see the mountain gorillas. Their expressions were slightly different. They looked sad. They looked how I did when I took the modem terminal out of the closet for the last time. Why did they look like that? Maybe if I lived in a cage forever, I would naturally look the same. But Hyeon-gyeong looked happy.

'Me, I really like gorillas. Like King Kong. I think it would be great to climb to the top of the Empire State Building with King Kong. Ann cried a lot when King Kong died in that movie.'

She said this with a childlike expression. So she was looking for a King Kong to carry her up the Empire State Building. The thrill of dizziness is like an orgasm, they say.

She was the only thing in the zoo that was really alive. She was like a little antelope, exploring every nook and cranny with a flurry of exclamations. No wonder I gave a short sigh when I looked at the hair shaking on the back of her head. Maybe I was just not vigorous enough. The animals in *Animal Kingdom* were so different from the animals in the zoo.

We went for dinner. While we were eating in the hotel's sky lounge, I gave her a tote bag by the designer she loved so much. How easy it was. I can't believe that all tastes can be compressed into a product number. I like the simplicity of famous brands. A serenade with a price tag. It would be difficult to express dreams and hopes more implicitly.

We spent that night in a room in the hotel. I must say it was better than I expected. We communicated by our bodies better than with words. Maybe I would pack a few more condoms next time, I was thinking, as I fell asleep with the lights off.

Just then, Hyeon-gyeong asked, 'Aren't you spending too much money on me? After all, you live alone. We could just meet at your home. I'm a good cook, too.'

I knew too much to rejoice. You shouldn't nibble at a delicious catch just because you're fishing. Sashimi can be really bad for you. I refused in the best possible way.

'Don't worry. It's not a waste of money if I spend it on you. That's how precious you are to me.'

And I actually acted like that. Dolce & Gabbana, Manolo Blahnik, Chanel, Tiffany, Cartier, Hermès, Louis Vuitton again. Other names followed once or twice a month. I had that much money. There was no other way to use it. Or rather, the more people I killed, the more my bank balance increased. I became a VIP at the bank and it grew increasingly unbearable every time I saw people grovelling before me. Oh, I've killed so many! Therefore, I wanted to spend money that way.

On the days when I went in to work, she would arrive with a present I had given her. And the things she owned that I could recognise increased. The bag she had always carried was replaced with other gifts I had provided. I was curious about two things. Were the clothes and shoes she'd worn previously fakes? And who the hell had given her the bag she always used to carry around?

Our relationship lasted about a year. In the meantime, I had bought her all kinds of things, but she had never taken me home, never introduced me to anyone, to her family or friends. There were many excuses. I worked nights, no one else knew what I did or how busy I was. She wasn't a fool either, so she knew what it all meant. I didn't want to admit it, but I couldn't be her King Kong. The name Hyeon-gyeong was too ordinary for her to live as the wife of a killer. She might understand that I could only buy luxury goods if I killed. But even if she accepted my job and compromised on buying new luxury goods with that money, I couldn't accept a woman who would accept killing people for her own satisfaction. I know this idea is self-contradictory. But I didn't want to live in a family overshadowed by murder.

One day, suddenly, there were no more calls from her. I didn't call back, like I always did. That's how it ended. There was no grand farewell scene, no plausible farewell ceremony. We met face to face at work every week and nodded lightly. That was all. I tried, but I could not read her expression. She had a very nonchalant face. She, being patient, might have finally realised my limitations and given up. Or maybe, as she had said – perhaps because I bought her a tote bag – she loved me with all her heart. That didn't make any difference. I always knew it would end like that, before it even started.

Addiction

It was shortly after my break-up with Hyeon-gyeong that the class president contacted me. I was surprised because I didn't expect to hear from anyone I had met at the reunion. My being beaten up in an alley that day had made a stronger impression on my companions in just five minutes than my entire high school days had done; we had not been close to each other in school and hadn't been in touch since graduation. He went on to work in a large company, had smooth promotions, a normal career. I was involved in the death of the chairman of his company, but he didn't know that. No matter how hard I tried to guess, I couldn't recall any reason why the class president should get in touch with me. Therefore, I suddenly wanted to meet him.

Meeting him again, he seemed unchanged except for a little more belly. He held out his hand with a nice smile. We shook hands. He took me to a nice place. It was one of the Apgujeong neighbourhood's wine bars, created by the sudden wine craze of recent years, low ceiling, dimly lit, the interior walls decorated with wood and red bricks, with bottles of wine piled up on cellar racks. It seemed a little strange to me, who rarely drank alcohol. Perhaps some people would call it some kind of style, but I, ignorant of such things, just liked the fact that it was dark.

'Nowadays, I've been craving some Burgundy wine.'

He ordered a wine with a long name that I cannot remember and added, 'Please give us the assorted cheese for the side dish, but without any goat's cheese.'

I remembered a day in autumn when I was a senior in high school. At the tripe restaurant where we had gathered to drink before the college entrance exam, the class president had ordered in just such natural tones. In his way of speaking, which seemed to show that he was familiar with this place, I felt a certain sense of separation as well as familiarity.

'You seem to know about wine?'

'Know? Business requires it. It's the same as it was in high school. If you didn't wear Nike, you were a dickhead, and now it's wine. Your company isn't like that?'

'Actually, I don't have to mix with my co-workers.' I shrugged.

'You're lucky. But if you want to be a part of office life, you have to know about things.'

I felt strange when he pronounced the words 'office life'. He went on about wines for a while. All of them seemed to have figured in the weekend issues of daily newspapers. I was grateful for his passionate readiness to talk about anything, because I had nothing to say, but I soon started to tire of it. Before I knew it, he had moved on to his dream wine.

'Really, if you put an '86 Château Mouton Rothschild, a '90 Château Margaux, and a 2000 Haut-Brion together for a tasting and savour the fragrance, talk about heaven ...'

Suddenly, I wondered just how much he really knew about those wines, with their names that were hard to remember.

'Have you ever tried any of the wines you've just mentioned?'

At that he smiled awkwardly.

'All that … is just common knowledge. Do I have to have tried them?'

'No, that's not what I'm saying …'

'I want to, of course. If ever I win the lottery, I'll buy some right away. Do you know how much one bottle costs?'

'No, I'm really ignorant. You seem to know a lot about them. I wonder what they taste like.'

'That's why you have to study wine. Think yourself lucky you asked me. If you'd said that somewhere else, you'd be ignored.'

I nodded instead of answering. He was right, I was the one who was weird. Some people know the top speed of a car they've never ridden in. It's not just about cars. We aspire to drink wines we've never tasted, to have audio equipment we've never owned, jewellery we don't have, clothes we can't wear, imagining that we'll enjoy such things one day.

As children, we dreamed of something happening, or of having some special ability. For example, we dreamed of things like dinosaurs or monsters, of the world being in danger, or of flying through the sky. Everyone spent time daydreaming of becoming a hero in their imagination, saving the Earth, discovering a secret princess. Reason took over at puberty. Celebrities on TV and the fascinating body odours of the opposite sex encountered on the bus always caused dizziness. And those things turned into a series of poignant stories or delusions that made our heads spin and led to fortuitous but fateful encounters, mournful, ardent love affairs. But at some point, everything started to change. Many of the narratives and characters began to turn into objects which were put into virtual shopping baskets on the internet, and then eventually the cancel button was pressed. Sometimes it was a house and sometimes it was a car. Or there were times when it was a famous brand. Anyway, the stories and characters were deleted. Things alone had meaning. The only stories adding to such fantasies were at best short and insignificant incidents like winning the lottery, or hitting the jackpot on the stock market. Where did all the narratives and characters disappear? The wine left a bitter aftertaste.

'But why did you contact me?'

'You know all about that kind of thing, don't you?'

'What?'

'Restructuring.'

It turned out that he was in charge of the interns who had started at his company that year. Three interns came in, all smart, learned the work quickly and did a great job. The interns were even better than his co-workers and subordinates, who were full-time employees. But now that their internship was over, he had to get rid of two of them. He wanted to know which ones to eliminate. And that's where he believed I could advise him, since I was a consultant on restructuring. I thought for a second. What advice could I give him? Essentially, the situation didn't seem much different from my usual work. I told him as plausibly as I could what I knew about restructuring.

'It doesn't matter which ones you eliminate. Is there one that you think might ruin the company? Or whose arrival means that the company will hit the jackpot? No matter what the HR department says, all you need is someone who will shut up and work. So do as you like.'

He nodded, looking very gloomy. 'That's true, but listening to you makes me feel like I don't want to go on with this job.'

'Then don't. You're not being held against your will.'

I was a little annoyed by his tearful voice. It wasn't a life-threatening thing for him to quit his job, unlike for me.

'Are you kidding? I have to pay this month's card bill, and I have to pay the instalments on my car. Besides, I signed up for life insurance last month and it's killing me.'

As an eighteen-year-old, I remembered, he had boasted that he would travel once he entered college. He said he would never be a salaryman, and would instead travel around the world writing travelogues. But now the furthest he went would be a nearby restaurant for lunch. He raised his glass with a gloomy look on his face.

'You're an expert at this, aren't you? Is that all you have to say?'

'Expert?'

I looked at the half-cut cheese on the plate. I recalled a few kinds of poison that are good to mix with cheese. If it came to being an expert, I was an expert.

'Just because we're called consultants, do you think we know anything about making cars, producing household appliances, constructing buildings? Companies hire us because nothing is decided by us, it's the result of consult-ing us, it's an objective assessment.'

Doubt clouded his face as he put down his glass.

'But it's not really objective at all, right?'

'Objective? Remember who makes all the data we refer to when we're being consulted. It's the company. Just because my value judgement doesn't enter into it doesn't mean it's objective.'

I no longer judge the good or bad side of my clients. They are just clients, nothing more.

'That means that the only reason you're being consulted is because you're not responsible.'

'Of course there are other reasons. It makes the people who pay believe that something professional and objective is going on. That's quite important. And we finish everything up very neatly and accurately.'

I thought about the people who had died from the plans I made. I knew them better than anyone else. But I shared no memories with them. Their health records were as well known to me as to their doctor, but I didn't know what they smelled like and had never felt their body's warmth. That is exactly what professionalism is.

'We can finish up calmly because our work is about other people. When we're tangled up like you, we get nervous and suffer from fear because we know those involved.'

'Fear? I worry about them because I pity them . . .'

'Or is it compassion? Surely the real reason why you don't want to do it is because you know your own situation isn't that different?'

Suddenly I realised I was saying this to myself. As I explained things to him, I vaguely realised the parallels to what I was doing. Consulting was like that after all.

'You'll end up talking about responsibility.'

'Yes, that's true,' he murmured, looking at the blood-coloured wine. 'I hate responsibility. Who the hell am I supposed to retain, and which ones to fire?'

Still he could choose the person, and that person wouldn't die. I envied him. So we emptied a bottle of wine from Burgundy, France. Now when tomorrow came he'd tell his boss the name of the one intern who should remain, and the other two would be fired. And I was going to get a document with personal information about someone to kill. That was the world we lived in.

We waited in the car park for a proxy driver to arrive. His car was pretty flashy. I let out a gentle exclamation out of courtesy, and in a voice full of pride he shyly said that there was still a year left on the instalments. Under the influence of the wine, he emphasised how stressful it was at work, and cautiously confessed that he was a TV home shopping addict. This month, he had bought three sets of marinated crab and some trousers, a steam cleaner and some raisin tree juice, and he couldn't help picking up his phone while he was watching TV. If that was all it took to forget his guilt about two young people who had pointlessly wasted six months of their lives, it was a small price to pay. I coughed lightly.

'Is your job worthwhile?' he asked.

'Well, restructuring means blowing someone away.'

'Companies are the same everywhere.'

'Yes, because it's the Company.'

'If our company ever needs to consult someone, I'll recommend you guys.'

'We're expensive. No joke.'

'It wouldn't cost me anything anyway.'

'It shouldn't happen to your company.'

'There are no exceptions if they think you're losing speed. It's ... .' He pretended to cut his throat.

Then the driver arrived.

He held my hand tightly and said, 'Thank you very much. I won't forget this favour.'

I laughed as I listened to words that were nothing more than a formal greeting. I wanted to say that I had recently restructured his chairman. At that moment, I realised why he had looked me up. It wasn't that he didn't know who to choose. He just needed someone to rationalise his actions. It was bitter to act as a villain for the self-justification of the ordinary.

I wanted to sleep with Hyeon-gyeong. But I didn't call her. I reflected that to me she was an addiction just like home shopping. Fake comfort. I remembered something I'd read one day. According to British scientists, the pleasure centres in the brain for sex, shopping and drugs are the same.

I envied him. I envied his shrewdness. It was the kind of thing that only ordinary people could have. Mediocrity seemed to shine so piercingly bright, at least at that moment.

The Envelope

Around this time, my relatives began to nag me more insistently every holiday. It was like a rite of passage for all unmarried people my age. I had already been thinking I should get married like everyone else when I started working in earnest, living away from my parents. But I always left it as a thought, because of my job. In the meantime, my age and the number of people I had killed both passed thirty. On holidays, everyone asked the same question tirelessly: 'When are you going to get married?' And I always answered 'Well . . .'

One day, I got a call from my mother. Speaking in an urgent voice, she said it was important, and when I went rushing out in my indoor slippers, I found her in front of a marriage bureau. I tried to turn away, but she dragged me in with a quick slap on the back. So the days began when I had to meet countless unknown women. The so-called couple manager dragged me out to meet a new woman almost every other week. It was the moment when the business card designed by the Company saw the light of day again.

At first, I felt like meat hanging in a freezer with its grade stamped on it. However, that feeling soon faded after mingling a few times with other pieces of meat. Compared to all the things that I had had to adapt to when becoming a killer, the feeling of being graded and sold was like light entertainment. It's fun to do anything after killing more people than your age. Thanks to the salary that death brought me, I met some nice women. No, let's correct that. I met some really nice women. They were all good enough to marry straight away, tomorrow. But there was something that made me hesitate. It was only after I met her that I knew what it was.

With the very pretty name Yerin, she was a sunnier version of my Manager. If my Manager was a perfect wet dream, Yerin was the complete fantasy. She was slender, elegant and mysterious, like an iris. Just looking at her as she spoke quietly, her head turned toward the window, filled me with happiness. From the moment we first met and talked, there was something about her that was different from other women. Others tried to check if I was right for them; whether the grade was properly stamped, so to speak, the meat firm and free of defects. Everyone was faithful to their purpose, there was nothing to complain about. That was why we were meeting after all. But I was getting tired of such meetings. It felt as if I kept meeting the same person with a different profile and different appearance. If someone claimed that the marriage bureau was creating and sending out clones, I would have believed it.

When I asked the couple manager secretly, she said with great pride, 'That's how strict the choice of candidates is. We're proud of our specialised database that can help you find the right spouse.'

When I heard that, I thought of my specialised database for murder. It's the same everywhere. But Yerin was different.

For example, the first thing she said to me was this. 'As I was on my way out, I passed a pool left by yesterday's rain, and I saw the blue sky reflected in it. How shall I put it? It was very refreshing.'

I'll never forget those words. We were drinking tea at a traditional tea house. Just looking at her holding up her teacup and putting it to her lips, I felt as if the top of my head was coming off. Her white hands lifted toward her mouth were soft and elegantly curved. The couple manager, seeing my expression, smiled an encouragement and quickly left us alone together.

I felt as though we had been dating for ages. Aside from the standard questions, we talked about the weather, Magritte's paintings and the best music to listen to on rainy days. At our second meeting, we exchanged CDs we had prepared of the music we'd talked about previously, and discussed a colleague of hers who had made her angry recently. She was five years younger than I was and, unable to overcome her mother's insistence, she had registered with the marriage bureau for the same reason I had. She was working on illustrations and had a white three-year-old cat named Azrael.

Once she called me late at night just to say, 'Flowers fall, but surely there are still phones.'

And once we talked about a painter and argued about whether art is more important than life.

She answered the question by saying: 'Though flowers bloom easily, to be beautiful is not easy.'

I reckoned I could talk about her in more detail than anyone I'd ever met, including the people I'd met and the people I'd killed. There was something mysterious about her, which constantly excited me every time we met. As if something was being hidden. Is there any other way of explaining that, apart from the word 'love'? Listening to the music she gave me, I remembered the names of the first and second children I had thought up in the military. I leaned against the window in the back of the bus and laughed foolishly.

The next day I went and chose a car. I hadn't needed a car before, because I hardly had to go out of the house. But I decided to buy a car so I could drive her home. I wanted to buy a car that she would love, so I found a brand that everyone admired. I'd already learned from Hyeon-gyeong that all tastes can be explained by brand names.

The interior of the store was cold, simple and colourful at the same time. Hyeon-gyeong had also told me that being able to unite two contradictory tendencies meant that a brand was high-end.

The dealer said, 'You know what? It's not just a car.'

He caressed the smooth body with one hand.

'When you ride this and get out somewhere, the air around you feels wrong.'

He said this in a proud voice. And it really was so. I could understand why the class president had accepted the burden of instalments and chosen a luxury car. If I wanted to change lanes, I could see the car behind me braking in the wing mirror the moment I turned on the blinker. Every time I stepped on the accelerator, the car lightly sped past all others. I was the king of the road. Buying a new car with a smooth European origin that, to borrow the dealer's expression, 'would make women wet their panties the moment you step on the brake' cost exactly the money I received from restructuring three people. But it didn't matter. There were plenty of people left to kill.

I sat in the new car and listened to the music she had given me. That alone seemed to fill my heart with warm light. Thanks to the rain not too long before, the leaves were all falling and we were entering winter. But everything looked green when I left the house.

There were days when we went together everywhere by car. Still now, on snowy days, I remember stopping the car on the banks of the Han River, where we listened to music and watched the water vanish under white snow. Her lips were so warm, and her skin was tender enough to make me want to cry. Her body shone white and everything else grew dim in the endless snow. And at some point she and I also faded from view as the windows steamed over.

Every moment we spent together was precious. It's still easy for me to think of her when I see rain falling, dark clouds clearing and the waning moon emerging. The music we listened to, the paths we walked along together, the smell of her flesh and her soft skin. They remain stamped inside me and come to mind almost as if I could touch them when I close my eyes. I was so happy that I was afraid. On my way home alone, I would park the car, smoke a cigarette and feel scared that it might all be a dream. Such were those precious days when I inevitably felt sad. Just remembering those moments now makes my fingertips tremble. Sometimes I have a deep regret, a wish that things could be reversed somehow. But I couldn't help myself, nor everything that followed.

It was only a few days before the start of spring that I decided to propose to her. One day, after a few early showers, the last cold snap came, and we spent the Sunday together. Naked apart from an apron, she made me bean paste stew. The small window in the kitchen was reflecting a mixture of the white snow that had fallen the day before and her white flesh. Looking at the bright sunlight, I thought, *I'm going to buy a ring just as bright tomorrow.*

* * *

The snow that had fallen two days before had melted and the streets were muddy. The white trainers I wore were a mess. In the past, I never left the house, so the weather didn't matter. Now, even a hundred years of cold weather couldn't stop me.

I spoke to the clerk. 'I'm thinking of proposing, so I want to see some rings.'

But what I was looking for wasn't a ring. It was the seed of the dreams I was nourishing. After a long thought, I bought a ring with a big diamond. Even at that moment, I hated myself for thinking that it was worth the same as one death. But every choice comes with a price.

The shape of the ring was a design in which diamonds stuck in the middle of two neat bands bloomed like flowers. When and how should I tell her? How could I make it an unforgettable proposal? I had a lot on my mind. Suddenly the ring felt heavy. What if she refused?

On the way home, I violated two traffic signals and took a wrong turning. When I managed to get home, there was a pair of black high heels on the porch. A visitor. I must have left the door unlocked when I went out. I entered, calling Yerin's name. She was the only person who could have come in. In the living room sat the Manager, wearing a black coat.

'There's a new job,' she said.

Something about this was odd. She had never before brought work to my house herself. For the first time I wasn't happy to see the face of the goddess of my wet dreams. I put on a bright voice to hide my feelings.

'Hey, I'll be rich. I've just come back from spending money, and now it's more work.'

She put an envelope down on the table.

'I know you're busy dating, but do it right.'

I replied, looking down at the envelope, 'Have I ever neglected anything? Why, is there a problem?'

'It's, it's not … This one's kind of a test.'

The Manager got up from her seat.

'A test? But I've already passed the test.'

I raised my voice without realising it. The Manager clicked her tongue as if I was being pathetic.

'Even the driver's licence that the state scatters around has to be renewed, so surely it's natural?'

'But you don't take the test again every time.'

'There are so many accidents for exactly that reason, because people don't take the test again every time. You know what the Company is like.'

She snorted and turned her eyes back to the envelope.

'Maybe it's hard, killing someone you know. But this person is in a bit of trouble.'

The Manager smiled. Suddenly, my mind went blank. An acquaintance? An acquaintance. The word was circulating in my head, destroying everything. The ring, the happiness of the last few months, the excitement, the bright times, all had been shattered by just a few words. I stood frozen, forgetting to take off my coat. When I came to my senses, the Manager had already left and only the envelope remained. It was neatly and clearly placed on the table.

Who might it be? Who might this person be, whom she said I knew? Which of the people I knew would I find difficult to kill? I tried to guess who might be indicated in the envelope. But I already knew. There was no need to worry. Because there was only one person who had been in and out of my house. The computer was full of documents that should not have been seen, and the locked closet still contained records of the last person killed.

I cleaned the whole house, washed the laundry and reorganised the drawers. I also tidied up all the records in the closet. But the envelope was still there.

I washed the dishes, threw away the food scraps left in the drain of the sink, washed the car and sorted the trash. Still, the envelope was there.

I sorted out the receipts I'd collected over the past four years, dismantled the computer, scrubbed the sink and drain hole. All the messy rubbish stimulated my diaphragm. I kept throwing stuff away. Still, the envelope was there.

If anyone asks me about despair, I'll answer that it's shaped like a light beige envelope. At least it was for me. It took me three days to open the envelope. Then it was not because I found the courage but because I was so afraid and distressed that I couldn't stand it anymore. I didn't make any rash decisions. Save her and I myself would die. I would not have been afraid if I had had such a wonderful conviction. But even if I risked my life to spare hers, if she really knew something she wasn't supposed to know, it would be no different than breaking a rock with an egg. I didn't think I could stop the Company just by trying. After all, I didn't even know the real identity of the Company.

I opened the envelope. There were papers. I stood them up and tapped them on the edge of the table. The weight of the neatly arranged documents felt too heavy. I turned over the first page. A picture. A familiar face. I stared into the eyes of the person who was to embrace death.

Original Sin

I once went to church when I was young. It was Christmas. If you think I went to church for the Christmas snacks, you must be a generation older than me. Having grown up in the early eighties, we were not interested in snacks or bread from the church unless we were very poor. If I had asked my friends to go to church because they were giving away snacks, I would have been told, 'No, let's go to an arcade and play *Galaga*.'

But I decided to go to church on a friend's suggestion. The reason Christmas was special to me was not because of the snacks or bread, but because that day was an exception.

Back then there used to be an announcement just before the news at 9 p.m.: against a backdrop of pictures of the moon and a sleeping child an announcer would say that good children should go to Dreamland – something that is not particularly funny, remembered now. As the social atmosphere reflected strictly such broadcasts, if and when children were outside beyond that time, adults would urge them to go home and sleep. They were in a similar situation because they couldn't go out after the curfew siren at midnight. A soldier, who would later claim to have only 290,000, won in assets, was running the country, so the whole population was run like an army.

One of the riddles I most wanted to know the answer to at that time was, what happened after midnight? And why did ghosts only come out at midnight? The reason why I had never seen any ghosts was because I had to go to bed at nine. Maybe the door to a four-dimensional world would open at midnight, as in the cartoon series *Paul's Miraculous Adventure*. I used to imagine that sometimes just before I fell asleep in a room with the lights turned off.

What makes adults prevent children from staying up late at night? I turned it over in my mind. What was the great secret that demanded that all children must go to sleep? I couldn't wait to become an adult. But time was hardly on my side. If someone talked about time, ten days were like a month, a year sounded like a decade. Ten years ahead, I felt it would never come.

But then I found out that I didn't have to wait that long. There was always an exception, and in this instance, it was Christmas. I got permission from my parents to stay up until the church service ended.

The church I went to for the first time was strange. I think there were various activities, such as playing, singing and celebrating Christmas. However, habit is a scary thing, so after nine o'clock, my eyelids were heavy and I couldn't stay awake. The chair was hard, but the church's uniquely boring and cosy atmosphere led me to Dreamland. Having dozed off, I was able to sleep soundly until just before midnight.

When midnight was around the corner, I opened my eyes to a booming voice. It was a pastor. The pastor was preaching in a loud voice that Jesus was crucified for our sins. He stressed that we cannot go to Heaven, therefore, unless we go to Jesus.

I wiped away the saliva around my mouth and asked the Sunday School teacher beside me in a low voice:

'Then someone who has never sinned goes to Heaven regardless of Jesus?'

The teacher looked around and replied in a similarly low voice:

'There's no one who hasn't sinned.'

'There's a lot of newborn babies and very nice people ... What did they do to deserve it?'

The teacher explained that Adam, the first ancestor of mankind, had sinned, so everyone who is a descendant of his has sinned from birth, and that is the original sin. It followed at the same time that existence itself was a sin. It sounded a little ridiculous to me. I tried to argue, but the teacher told me to be quiet and stop talking when the pastor was preaching. I stood up after muttering, 'You've talked more than I have.' I could feel everyone's eyes on me. But I went out of the church, leaving those eyes behind. Because that was not what I wanted to know.

The streets were quiet, and the night air was very cold. The remains of my drowsiness blew away in the cold winter wind. From somewhere I could hear the loud voices of drunkards and the barking of dogs. And I heard a bell ring from a church. It was ringing midnight. I stopped in my tracks. My heart was pounding. I smiled.

But that was all. There was nothing mysterious about it. The street was quiet again once the bell stopped. The barking of dogs died down and people's footsteps faded away, but that was it. Time did not stop, as in the cartoon, there were no large bats filling the sky, no maiden ghosts, no werewolves and no ghosts of unmarried men in white robes. Then why did adults force us to go to bed early? I suddenly became angry. Midnight was special because it was a forbidden time. That was all.

Christmas quickly became boring once I realised that the world was no different after midnight. If there were no ghosts, no doors to the four-dimensional world, no magic time, then it was clear that there would be no Santa. My feelings were complex, and I couldn't explain it well at the time. It was only when I was much older that I realised I'd felt like I was being made a fool of.

My mother asked me if church was boring, and I just said yes. And I fell asleep after drinking some warm cocoa. When I woke up, there was a gift from Santa Claus at my bedside.

Inwardly I snorted – *humph* – exclaiming, 'Wow! Has Santa Claus really paid a visit?'

Everything grew boringly serious after that. In the New Year, the curfew disappeared and the stupid Dreamland broadcasts ended. *Galaga* was also replaced by *Xevious*. In the new semester, buying collections of books spread like a fever, and for middle-class people, a collection of world literature and an encyclopaedia were essential. My family bought the complete Sherlock Holmes stories. Crime and detectives occupied the world of magic and adventure and the place where Santa had gone.

So everything changed, but the concept of original sin sometimes came to my mind. Existence itself as sin. *Why is existence itself a sin? Why do mature adults believe such nonsense?* The words came to my mind on cold nights as I grew older, passed puberty and edged past thirty.

It was only after the trip to the Democratic Republic of the Congo that I found out. And I went to the DRC entirely because of the beige envelope of my despair. Of course, at the time, I didn't know that I would go to the DRC or discover the answer to my questions.

* * *

The person in the document was not the illustrator. Thankfully, my prediction had been wrong. But I didn't shed tears of joy. Because the Manager hadn't lied. The target was Hyeon-gyeong. At first I felt something like relief. I think I was even a little bit pleased. Then came a moment of confusion. I didn't know if I could call it a relationship, but she was a girl I had dated. So I felt uncomfortable. We did see the gorillas at the zoo together. There were many things I learned while meeting with her. Things like the style and symbolism of the brands that create so-called luxury goods. They looked the same to me, but they had incredibly different meanings. It was a new world of allusions, metaphors and show-offs. But that wasn't reason enough not to kill her. The sex between us was really good, but it wasn't great enough to make me want to risk my life. What's more, I was not even in a position to decide whether she should live or die.

I thought I'd look on the bright side. Yerin was at least alive, and I could propose. It would be regrettable if an unlucky ex-lover was in an accident, but it would be better for Hyeon-gyeong than ending up in pain at the hands of others. Anyway, our relationship had not been close enough to call ourselves lovers.

I spread out the papers and reconstructed Hyeon-gyeong's daily life. Most of the things I knew about her daily life only applied to one day a week, so this felt a little weird. I got to know her family better than when I was seeing her for all that time.

Her family was very poor. Her father was out of work and her brother was working in a factory. Probably her mother, who worked at a market, had raised the children. Poverty must surely have been worse than having a terribly ordinary name. Just looking at the documents gave me the picture. For Hyeon-gyeong, brands must have been a way to prove that she was a much cooler person than she really was. Suddenly, I wondered what it was the Manager thought I didn't need to know.

It was not hard to guess. Hyeon-gyeong was an accountant and must have found something odd while examining the office's cash flow. I felt a little sad that sincerity was the cause of her death. Perhaps only the gifts I gave her and the bag she carried from the beginning were real luxury goods. Imagine her doing all that footwork and getting paid to buy imitations, knowing they were fakes. It reminded me of the closet in her small semi-basement room with such things hanging in it. It was quite a sad sight. But what was sadder in her closet were the things I had bought her. What on earth could Louis Vuitton prove in a semi-basement rented room?

Setting aside all feelings, I planned step by step. It's not easy to kill a young person, because there are not many kinds of death to choose from. Young deaths are usually terrible. Although the contrast between youth and death is partly to blame, it is mainly because there is no possible cause of death other than a dreadful accident. Older people have many diseases and take a lot of medications. Also, people tend to accept their deaths easily. The work involved is at a totally different level of difficulty. Fortunately, young people rarely own enough to make them subject to such requests. Our work is too expensive to simply eliminate the weak. There is a clear class difference in the service of death, capitalist society being what it is. Most of the people I had given a natural death to were in their forties at least.

She was an acquaintance and a person I had slept with. Therefore I didn't want to give her a hideous and painful death. I analysed her data closely. Thanks to that, I solved a small, long drawn-out question. It was the branch manager who had presented her with her first bag. The relationship between the two seemed to have been quite serious until just before we met, or before she first slept with me. Finding this out was not very pleasant. But thanks to this, I lost a lot of my reluctance while planning. And I remembered one fact that I needed for her to die naturally.

Suicide is a relatively neat death for someone young. One of the common misconceptions about death is the idea that suicide is easy to disguise. If the investigators and the coroner can be bribed, it might be possible to disguise a suicide. Otherwise, it is very difficult. This is because the body itself testifies to death. If a person whose death someone tries to disguise as a suicide resists at all, there will be signs of that resistance on the body. It's better if drugs are used, but in that case, the dead person must have had a habitual drug addiction or a corresponding medical history. Just try obtaining a hundred sleeping pills without a prescription. Moreover, I would like to ask how to feed a hundred sleeping pills to someone without resistance. In the United States it might be possible to use stimulants like crack cocaine. Toss some of the drug around, put a syringe in an arm and it will be simple enough. However, if someone dies like that in Korea, a drug task force will immediately investigate thoroughly, even digging up the floors. In the end, such suicides are not suicides, but suspicious deaths.

What about disguising strangulation? Always provided that experienced people are involved, it is not difficult to distinguish between strangulation caused by suicide and strangulation caused by murder. From the method of pressing to the direction of the hands, the location of the strangulation marks and the posture of the body as it was found will all testify whether it was suicide or not. Other methods are similar. From cutting the veins in a bathtub to death by falling, it is rarely as easy to disguise suicide as in movies.

In the case of Professor Choi Jong-gil, whose death had been claimed to be a suicide by the Central Intelligence Agency, even they failed to disguise it as a fall, supposedly the easiest way to cover up a suicide. If a murder is mistakenly concluded to have been a suicide, it is usually not because the person who planned it is competent, but because the person who investigated it is incompetent. Of course, I might be lucky with the murder I planned, but relying on luck alone would make it hard to avoid embarrassing the Company. I always postulate the worst-case scenario. That way, I can handle things perfectly.

Anyway, that's how hard it is to disguise suicide. If there were any cases where I disguised the deaths as suicide, they were cases where a customer suffering from depression hid a suicide note somewhere in a drawer or had a medical record of depression as long as a broadcasting station schedule. In such cases, both the bereaved family and the police can easily understand the death. Otherwise, even the smallest aspect of the cause of death is suspected by the bereaved. Imagine if a close friend or a loved one dies. You wouldn't be able to believe it at first, if a friend you met yesterday and joked with suddenly committed suicide. And you would feel responsible. Maybe you could have prevented it. If the pain of responsibility becomes too great, people begin to believe that it was not suicide. Then they sniff about everywhere, desperately searching for clues – not to save the person who is already dead, but to save themselves from suffering. Unless all the manipulation of evidence is as systematic as possible, there is no way of stopping the bereaved family from smelling it out.

That's where I was lucky. Hyeon-gyeong habitually took anti-depressants. She took her medicine as if she was chewing gum after meals, claiming that it made her happy. Of course, she had to go to the hospital to get the medicine, but that didn't seem to matter.

'It's not difficult. I just need to tell them that I don't want to live with this look on my face.'

Hyeon-gyeong once frowned as she swallowed the medicine, a ridiculous look on her face. I thought she was right. It was only natural that in my indifference I did not once try asking her more about this. In a corner of her luxury bag were small capsules full of uppers, and when they entered her brain, they flashed and brought her vitality and happiness. There was no fairy wand as in *Cinderella*. I was always confused whether her lifestyle was so simple and straightforward because of the medicine or whether she had to take medicine because of her lifestyle, but now it was her turn to earn me some money.

Statistically, the time when people suffering from depression commit suicide is the moment they are recovering. They think they've improved a lot and stop taking the pills. Then the brain screams for dopamine and depression comes sweeping back like a tidal wave. In the end, such people choose suicide instead of medicine. My plan was simple. Fill an empty medicine bottle with pills, put her to sleep with chloroform, and hang her. Police would then think she'd stopped taking the pills and based on long experience, they'd conclude it was suicide.

But at the time I was overlooking one thing: my relationship with her. The police were certain to investigate me if something ever happened to her.

The End of Paradise

The Travels of Marco Polo tells the story of the Old Man of the Mountain and the Assassins. The Old Man of the Mountain created a paradise for assassins, and at the same time used the paradise to direct assassinations.

An old man named Alaodin of Mulehet lived in a beautiful and magnificent palace on a mountain and was praised by the people nearby for his noble and devout faith. He did not deny the rumours. He actually owned his own paradise.

He created a secret garden in a valley between two mountains that no one but himself and the assassins he wanted to send into the world could enter. In the garden stood the most beautiful house imaginable: the garden literally was flowing with milk and honey, and the table was full of all kinds of delicacies. And among the flowers and fruit trees in the garden were beautiful ladies dressed in gold and silk, who knew all the coquettish arts and finesse that pleased men.

If you lived in that region at that time, were healthy enough and had a firm faith in Allah, you might suddenly wake up there, a small paradise created on earth. The miracle would occur shortly after meeting the old man, chatting lightly about God and drinking the drink he gave you. All the beautiful women there would love you, obey you, and everything you wanted would be yours. There were also all sorts of rare hallucinogenic drugs and hash-ish, which would make the little paradise before your eyes look even more vivid and heavenly. As the smoke rose, time faded, unhappiness was banished from paradise. At last you had found heaven. Until the old man had someone he wanted to kill.

The endless pleasures and unlimited happiness would end suddenly one day. Waking on the cold floor of the old man's palace, you don't understand what has happened. Shivering with withdrawal symptoms, you feel the unbear-able loss of heaven, vanished from before your eyes. In a trembling voice, you explain to the old man the incredible things that you saw. The old man replies to you, who are now banished from Paradise like Adam, explaining that it was what the Prophet Muhammad had called Paradise. You may want to die. Your brain screams for hashish, and your body binds you to the floor, gripped by gravity like a giant pendulum. The only reason you can't kill yourself is because you know that suicide is a sin and that if your kill yourself you can't go to Paradise.

The old man says, holding your hand trembling with a desire for Heaven, or from withdrawal symptoms, 'He will send down grace.' The grace is as follows. 'There's someone who is disobeying the teachings of the Prophet Muhammad. If you kill him, you'll come back here and be rewarded with Paradise. If you fail or die in the process, your soul will go to a place beside the Prophet Muhammad.'

You listen to the old man and don't hesitate. The kind old man will throw a big feast for you before you leave. Maybe he'll give you a little hashish to still your trembling hand. So you cross the desert in order to return to the paradise from which you have been exiled.

Many dreamy nights and days intersect in the sand-storms, shadows overlap, from Paradise to Hell, from Hell to Paradise, and this is how the short story of a young assassin begins, ending in psychedelic smoke, a scimitar and red blood.

The Mulehet region in *The Travels of Marco Polo* does not actually exist. Mulehet is the plural form of Mulahida, meaning 'pagan'. That is another name for the Ismailis, who believe in a seventh imam, a belief that has disappeared among other branches of Shia Islam. This story, which sounds like a novel, actually happened. It is, of course, somewhat exaggerated.

The real history is harsher and colder. There was a young man named Hassan-i Sabbah. The young man, who was originally a Shiite, had been caught in a fight with the Sunnis and was being pursued. One day, as flight and escape continued, he met some Ismailis and was influenced by them. Believing in the seventh imam, they were ostra-cised not only by Sunnis but also by the small number of Shiites who considered the twelfth imam as their saviour. Therefore, something more powerful was needed to spread and protect their faith. At first it was a fortress. Hassan-i Sabbah, who became the head of the Ismailis, realised that a large rocky mountain called Alamut could become a natu-ral fortification, and built two strongholds in nearby valleys and mountains in order to spread their faith in the region around. But their enemies were too strong, too many. So they chose to achieve maximum effect with a minimum number of people. They trained young people full of faith and devotion and sent them to the bedrooms of those who oppressed them. It was the moment when the world's first secret assassination squad was born.

Alamut was far from being a paradise, unlike how it appears in *The Travels of Marco Polo*. It was an extremely ascetic and religious place, almost like a monastery. In fact, Hassan-i Sabbah's own son was executed for drinking wine. Hassan's followers could not receive medical treatment because they were living in a remote area. Hassan, a brilliant strategist, religious leader and scholar, created drugs to treat them. Of course, those drugs included painkillers such as hashish. Over time, the rumours about the insidious assassins, together with the painkillers they used, turned into legend.

Later, the Order of the Assassins, the religious group that was to be an inspiration for the Taliban, turned into a political force after the appearance of Sinan Rashid al-Din, who is called the Old Man of the Mountain in *The Travels of Marco Polo*. At that time, Alamut was under the influence of the Crusaders. For the Ismailis, although they were Muslims, too, the Sunnis who were repressing them would not have seemed much different from the Christians. Indeed, as the saying goes 'the foe of my foe is my friend', so they joined forces with the Christians. They paid protection money to the Christians, and were often hired to assassinate Muslim leaders. Religion had already shifted down their priorities and they killed to maintain their sphere of influence and earn money. They even fought Saladin, who drove out the Christians.

There were several assassination attempts on this legendary Islamic leader and all of them were their workmanship. Saladin, of course, sought revenge. There was an expedition, and the punitive force reached the fortress, but Alamut was truly a natural stronghold, as Hassan-i Sabbah had seen. Until the Mongols, whom no one could stop, appeared and set fire to Alamut, they were notorious for almost two hundred years, a mixture of rumour and legend everywhere in the East and West.

There was double betrayal and death in the fall of the Assassins. When the sword of the Mongols, who had destroyed their old enemy, the Abbas dynasty, was directed at them, their chief, Rukn al-Din, surrendered, believing in their promises of cooperation and protection. Of course, despite the betrayal of their chief, the Assassins of Alamut resisted to the end. Alamut was besieged and falling little by little, while Rukn al-Din was indulging in hospitality and pleasure in the castle. Alamut was a natural fortress, but the head of the fortress was shouting out its secrets, and no defences could stop the Mongols at that time. The Mongols literally trampled down the home base of the Assassins they despised. And the traitor, Rukn al-Din, was horribly killed at the same time as Alamut fell. Mongolians could not leave behind the seeds of a disaster that might come to their bedrooms.

It is said that the name 'Assassin' originated from 'hash-ishi'. And 'hashishi' is commonly used to refer to habitual users of hashish. Of course, some say 'Hashishi' refers to the followers of Hassan-i Sabbah.

* * *

It was natural for me to have an uncomfortable relation-ship with Hyeon-gyeong. It was already an uncomfortable relationship to begin with, but now it had become much more uncomfortable. She seemed to think differently. She called me as I was on my way home from work one day and suddenly said: 'Let's go eat together.' Maybe this kind of thing didn't matter to her. Because it was little restaurants that gave her happiness. They were truly her Alamut. Her request made me feel awkward. But I couldn't say no. It sounds ridiculous but I wasn't tough enough to turn down a request from someone who was going to die by my own plan. I don't know if my clumsy good faith is the bigger fault.

She was as cheerful as ever, and she talked merrily about the time she had spent since we'd broken up. There was nothing special. Although I hesitated several times to ask a more pointed question, it was mostly casual talk, about cleaning the house while she was taking a break from work because she was not feeling well, although I had noticed no vacuum cleaner during our meetings at her house. And even more so now, I already knew the things she would never say. No matter how bright her voice was, it felt depressing when she spoke joyfully. Had she really grabbed me on a work day simply to talk about these things? I was annoyed.

But there was another reason why I was really angry. The main reason I couldn't stand being with her was because I had sent a plan for her natural death to the Company's postbox just the day before. It was a pretty neat plan and at least the body would be intact. I was quite satisfied. I had put a stamp on it and held her funeral in my heart. So here she was, already dead, and to me this was a bizarre meal with the dead. The food was like rubber and the seat was a pincushion. Unable to bear it any longer, I stopped eating and put down my spoon and chopsticks.

'Why did you ask me to have dinner with you?'

'Why? Aren't we allowed to eat together anymore?'

The mannequin-like smile disappeared from Hyeon-gyeong's face.

'It's not that ...'

I couldn't give a reason. She was the one who was going to die. She stared me in the face and suddenly spoke.

'I'm thinking of leaving the office.'

My already complicated head started to get even more complicated. Why was she telling me this? Why was she quitting? Did she know something and want to get away from the Company? Was this a threat to me?

'Why on earth ...'

'I'm getting bored with it.'

It was an inexplicable answer. Bored? What was boring about it? My instincts were sounding an alarm, telling me to get out of this situation. Obviously, something was not right. An ominous premonition of how much she knew spread in my mind's eye, like a burning ember falling on a reed bed. It seemed clear that if it was left alone, everything would blaze up. But the problem was that I didn't know where it had fallen. For heaven's sake, did she know I planned to kill her?

'Can't we go back to the way things used to be?'

I automatically frowned at her words. And she didn't miss the look on my face. Ah, I was sorry, but it was too late. I should have realised when she said she wanted to eat together. She came to me not because she knew something or wanted something, but just because she wanted me. Honestly, I wasn't in a bad mood. The fact that there was someone who wanted me, it was flattering ... But she was going to die. And even if she didn't die, I couldn't have chosen her. It occurred to me that I should be honest. Whatever she knew, she was soon going to be silent for good.

'There's someone I love,' I told her. 'I'm going to propose soon.'

For a moment, Hyeon-gyeong had a mysterious look on her face. It was a subtle impression that was hard to categorise, not sorrow, anger or resignation. Obviously, she didn't look very happy.

'I don't care if there's someone else.'

She spoke coldly. The moment I heard her words, I felt relieved. She wanted to enrich the collection in the closet a little bit. That was it after all. Sleep together, buy luxury goods, simple procedures. But I couldn't see her again. I was engaged in true love and didn't want to tarnish it.

'Let me know if you need anything. I'll do anything for you. But you know. We can't go back to how it was before.'

She smiled. It was a taut smile.

'It's not about that sort of thing. I just ...'

It didn't make any difference. Whatever she said, I wanted to end this long, breathtaking conversation. Clearly, if I didn't draw the line, she wouldn't give up. It didn't matter if I hurt her. I cut her off. And I spoke brutally.

'Don't think I'm the branch manager.'

Were those tears around her eyes? Hyeon-gyeong shook her head very briefly and energetically, as if she was trying to shake something off, and replied in a cheerful voice, 'Let's not talk about this anymore.'

But I could tell. I didn't know what I'd done to her. She was sitting there with a face like a dead person. But I couldn't help it. She'd always been the one who had the hang of things while we were meeting. She knew the line I had drawn more precisely than anyone else and had never crossed it. Why was she doing this now? What the hell did she know?

It didn't take long to realise this was the wrong question. What really mattered was not what she knew, but what I didn't know. I was asking the wrong question all along. But the really sad thing is that either way her fate wouldn't have changed much. The Company's decision was made and things were rolling downhill.

A week later she committed suicide as scheduled. It's awkward to say it was on schedule, but it was in any case. It was actually a little earlier than I expected. It usually took around fifteen days for the Company to carry out my plans. I thought it was obvious that the Company was very impatient, whatever she knew. I was wrong there, too.

Investigation

It was my day to go in to the office, and she hadn't been seen since morning. On the instructions of the branch manager, the staff called her house and mobile phone several times, but no one answered. My heart pounded every time. I was already guessing what must have happened. It was after lunch that her mother contacted the branch manager. Everyone in the office was surprised because Hyeon-gyeong had never looked like a suicidal person. I stood awkwardly among people with shocked expressions. Then the branch manager called me. I went into his room.

He was crying. He stared at me with red, bloodshot eyes.

'You didn't have to do that!' he said.

He knew something. He knew the Company was responsible and he knew what she knew. I was embarrassed by his aggressive attitude.

'I don't know what you're talking about.'

'Lies, I know what you two have been up to.'

I frowned.

'However Hyeon-gyeong died, it has nothing to do with me.'

He sounded like a child on the verge of tears while he was talking. What was Hyeon-gyeong to him? How had he felt when she chose me? It was clear that he believed it was love. But even if Hyeon-gyeong had wanted him to, he would never have divorced. He wasn't that kind of person. If such a thing was love, Hitler was Jesus.

'Hyeon-gyeong she just wanted to find out about you, that she loved you, wanted to know you better. I warned her. I told her that I didn't know you, that you were danger-ous. How much could she know, if she knew anything. What did she know?'

'You'd better think carefully about your way of speaking.'

I turned my back and slowly left the branch manager's room. There was nothing more to say. I really didn't know what Hyeon-gyeong knew. It wasn't her sincerity or her mistakes that had made her the target of the Company. She had been digging into my background. I remembered the last meal we had together. Why had she done such a foolish thing? She had said nothing, even though it was the best moment to blackmail me with whatever she'd found out.

Only then did I realise that something was very wrong. After our break-up, there was something important miss-ing to give consistency to her behaviour. I knew people were driven by desires. What was her desire? I stood in front of the branch manager's door and thought about her purpose in a way I hadn't before. Then I got a call from the police station.

The detective told me it was a formality. Still, my heart trembled. People who have lived steadily without break-ing the law are bound to be nervous when they go to the police station. At that time, given my deep involvement in the deaths of many people older than myself, the call could hardly be welcome.

From the moment I entered the door, I could feel my pulse accelerating. In my head, ominous imaginings pursued one another. I wondered if the branch manager had spilled something to the police or if the Company had abandoned me and made me a scapegoat. The branch manager was not that kind of person and the Company wouldn't go through such a cumbersome procedure if it wanted to get rid of me. I knew it in my head, but when I was sitting in the police station, I couldn't stop my hands sweating. I took a deep breath so I wouldn't betray any fear.

The detective looked tired. He asked questions as perfunctory as the term 'perfunctory procedure' suggests. He asked if she had shown any signs of suicide, and I said I didn't know. I told him we'd already split up, so I wouldn't have noticed any signs. He asked me how long it had been since we broke up, and I replied that it had been a little over half a year. And as I answered, I felt the continuing anxiety I had been feeling ever since I was called by the police. It didn't make sense that the police knew we were dating. It had been more than half a year since we'd broken up and no one knew about our relationship. Maybe she had told her family? The police, hearing the story through her family, must have found my contact information on her mobile phone. But in that case the family would have contacted me directly.

I sat up straight. The detective asked me if I was uncomfortable. I replied with a rather sad look that I couldn't believe she had done that. At that moment, a sneer flashed across the detective's face. It was an ominous sign. He was quite polite, but he knew something I didn't know. And because of that, the detective must have negative feelings about me. I swallowed reflexively, feeling a twitch of anxiety in my mouth like a pimple on my tongue. He asked when was the last time I saw her. I said it was a week before. He asked why we had met, and I explained that she had said she wanted us to meet again. The detective sighed and tapped the keyboard silently. I opened my mouth after coughing carefully.

'Is there something wrong?'

He replied with a pathetic look on his face after turning away from me to face the monitor.

'Yes, something's wrong. A person died.'

The detective looked sick and tired. I came up with the statistics. Around thirty people commit suicide each day around the country. Nearly twenty-five kill themselves every year for every 100,000 people. Perhaps the police have to deal with suicides every day, and even if they take turns, they will have to deal with them at least three or four times a month. I chose the simplest answer.

'I can't believe it. She looked fine a week ago.'

'Everyone says so. That attitude ends up ignoring the possibility of suicide.'

He snorted without taking his eyes off the monitor. He was criticising me. What was the problem and what should I be angry about here, and what might look suspicious if I didn't get angry?

I replied with a resentful expression. 'It's been over half a year. Why should I be called here because she hanged herself?'

His hands stopped. He raised his head. Then he frowned at me. My heart started beating again. I realised I had said something wrong. He raised an arm.

'What?'

He turned his arm sideways and pretended to dive.

'She jumped. Off the Han River Bridge. She didn't hang herself.'

Something that had been pursuing me was slowly collapsing with a loud crack. According to my plan, she was supposed to hang herself. The Company had never done anything differently than planned.

Seeing my expression, the detective asked, 'What? Because it's terrible to imagine? What's your problem? It's been half a year since you broke up.'

He took out a cigarette and lit it. My eyes were following his movements automatically, but in my head I was thinking like crazy, trying to understand how things were unfolding. She had jumped into the Han River. That's not a bad method, so long as there are no signs of a struggle. However, if there is no suicide note and no clear reason for suicide, there is a risk of an autopsy being held if the body is found after jumping. Why had the Company handled things this way? The detective, who had been inhaling deeply after lighting up the cigarette, exhaled a cloud of smoke as he spoke.

'I see it as murder, damn it. No matter what the law says.'

I closed my eyes tightly. Finally, the anxiety that I had felt instinctively from the moment I entered the police station had begun to reveal its true form. Suddenly, no matter what happened in the future, I thought it would be better not to talk. Should I call a lawyer first?

'It's not just being stabbed with knives and being hit that kills people.'

Every word made me dizzy as if my blood was flowing down into my feet. *That's it. Will the Company help me? I know a lot of things, so the Company won't stay inactive. Then I can escape. The Company can do anything.* I kept muttering in my mind to calm myself down. But I couldn't control my trembling.

'You look as though you have a conscience. Read it, since the bereaved family want you to see it, too.'

I opened my eyes. He was pushing a white envelope toward me.

'The investigation is over, you can go now.'

I looked at him with a puzzled look on my face. The detective was putting out the cigarette with a tired look on his face.

'You didn't know this would happen. You surely didn't want it. Fate, really ... Off you go.'

With the detective's sympathetic eyes following me, I left the police station carrying the envelope. Sitting in the car, I tried to calm my staggered heart. I had thought it was all over. What the hell happened? I opened the envelope and took out the paper. Familiar handwriting caught my eye. It was almost like Hyeon-gyeong's handwriting. 'Mum, I'm sorry.' As soon as I read the first phrase, I realised that it was a suicide note. This, too, was not part of the plan. What the hell was the Company doing? A suicide note? I wanted to know what the idiot was thinking, risking a handwriting test.

I read her suicide note slowly. It was full of ridiculous stories. I laughed. I laughed so hard that I cried. There was no reason to cry. It was a hoax. The Company must have hired someone else. The idiot had made her jump to her death and had even fabricated a suicide note. Unless the coroner was an idiot, he would not miss the marks on her wrists or back when he pushed her with his foot. I couldn't believe they'd handled it like this. They were lucky not to be caught. I couldn't stop crying at the thought of how many people would die that day because of incompetent human beings in the judicial system. It really showed a lack of professional skill. But that a stupid detective and a pathetic coroner missed all the evidence and concluded it was suicide, I couldn't believe it.

The Suicide Note

Mum, I'm sorry. I'm very sorry. I know how you feel. It's so painful when your child dies. Yeah, you can't believe it, but I know how it feels. That's why I'm even more sorry.

But please know, it's a hard decision. I've been thinking about it for a long time. And I've been waiting. It'll get better over time. That's what I believed. But it just got harder and harder to bear. I can hardly sleep at night anymore. It's too tough. There really was no other way.

As a matter of fact, I lied. About him. The story that we're getting married soon. It's all a lie. We broke up. A long time ago. I met him five days ago and asked him if we could meet again, but I was rejected. He knew about it. How I used to be. I really wanted to die there.

Don't blame him, though. Because I really was happy. He's a good man. I still remember the first day we ate together. I've never been to such a wonderful place before. I didn't know what to do, but he taught me kindly. I'm not mad at him. I was intimidated just by being there, but he told me it was okay. And when he said he was always looking at me, I almost cried. I was so happy. I felt like I had become a very special person. And we went to the zoo together. You know

I couldn't even go to the zoo, because I couldn't attend the school picnics. He said that to me that day: 'You're a precious person.' Why didn't time stop then? I wish it had.

He really valued me the whole time. You know how my ex-boyfriends used to treat me. I've never seen a man like that before. I remember what wonderful gifts he bought me every time, and I was really happy but scared. Looking at the presents he gave me alone in the middle of the night, it felt like they were telling me: 'You don't belong with him.'

I called him a couple of times, but you know. He's working American time. It's always been a distraction. I realised it every time. Someone like me, how unhelpful that is. But it was fun to meet. I couldn't see him often because he was busy, but I felt like the whole world was mine while we were together.

But I've always been afraid. I always felt like he was looking somewhere else. He would be listening to what I said, and always be kind, but lacking something. At first, I thought there might be another woman. But there wasn't. It's silly, but I stood on guard in front of his house once after work. No one came to his house. He was just as lonely as I was. Every time we were together, I shouted in my heart: *Look at me.* And I thought, he is looking at you. It's just your anxiety.

But on the nights we spent together, sometimes he was as cold as a corpse. I once asked why. He answered with a smile: 'It's not going to happen.' But I knew, too. That he had a secret. Because he was always hiding something from me. I thought about what the secret was. *He doesn't love you.* That's the secret.

Once I started doubting, I couldn't stop. I was out of my mind. I thought about him all day and it was always painful when he didn't come in to work. It was then that I started going to the hospital. The doctor said: 'Try talking to him.' But I couldn't tell him. If he said something and it was irreversible … it was my first happiness and I couldn't end it like that. So I started taking medicine. You don't know how heartbroken I was when he asked about the medicine. I'm still bruised, but it's silly to take medicine. But if it could have lasted forever, I would have been happy to keep doing so.

Then I missed my period. I thought, I'm not calling until he calls first. If he calls, he loves me. Then I'll tell him. He'll be happy with this news and we'll get married. But I didn't get a call. I wasn't disappointed. I was expecting it. I've told you this before. He doesn't like to call. So I changed my goal. Every time I met him in the office once a week, I waited for him to ask me why I hadn't called him. Then I'd tell him why. Then…

A week passed like that. I thought, he must have been busy. Another week passed. Something must have happened. And another week. Yeah, we had a holiday last week. Believe it or not, I didn't think I'd ask for that stupid reason. But whenever he saw me at work, he greeted me casually with a look that said nothing had happened. As if there was nothing between us.

So I went to the hospital. It was really good. Because I was angry at the time. I sold the necklace he bought me to the gold and silver shop because I didn't have any money. I was really surprised. It was much more expensive than I thought. I couldn't understand. If there was nothing between us, what was he thinking when he gave this to me as a gift? It didn't matter.

It's a nothing of a child born out of a nothing-between-us relationship.

It was a day after rain had fallen. The sky was really clear. I came out of the hospital, took my medicine and thought: *It's okay, nothing has happened.* I didn't even cry. There was no reason to cry.

But I couldn't sleep. I couldn't go to the hospital and ask for sleeping pills. If I asked for sleeping pills while I was already getting other medicine, they'd ask why. I wasn't going to tell anyone, ever. It was a secret I would take to the grave.

So I stayed awake all night long every day. Every night I pulled out all the gifts he had given me and put them in a box. When dawn came, I was going to burn them all before going to work. But when the sun came up, I put them all back in place, feeling exhausted.

And there was him. You can't begin to imagine how much I hated him when he didn't change in the slightest. I hated him so much that I wanted to kill him. Every time I saw him, my stomach grew knotted with uncontrollable emotions. I wanted to know why he had acted like that. What had made him so kind to me, and what made him abandon me.

That's why I followed him. And I figured out why. He'd got a new woman. If he had another woman, I was going to die with him or kill her, but the moment I saw her, strangely, I wasn't angry. You see, she was a woman like every brand I've ever loved. She was everything I ever admired, everything I wanted to be. How can that be? I'm not angry, I'm sad. Oh, no wonder I ended up like this. You know what's funny? She looked like someone in the pamphlets mailed out every month from department stores; she was rich enough to buy anything she wanted, but she only wore things that weren't worth half the price of a single watch I had. She was so good-looking that she didn't have to wear anything expensive. Besides, she hadn't killed anyone. I even killed my baby.

It must have been around this time that I started to hear the baby crying when I was lying alone at home. I was scared at first. And I took medicine. But whenever I fell asleep I could hear the baby crying.

One snowy night, I couldn't stand it and ran out of the house. I came out without any warm clothing and wearing only slippers, though it was snowing heavily. I couldn't see properly, I had come so far, my feet were cold and my shoulders were cringing. The cold penetrated deep into my lower abdomen and my teeth were knocking together. I screamed in the alley where I heard the crying. 'Stop it! Stop it! Please stop!' Then the crying stopped. I slipped and fell as I turned around. I was feeling colder because of the snow that had piled up. As I lay there, face down, I realised that my baby was crying because it was cold.

I was a stupid mother because I didn't realise that. Well, I was the one who killed the baby. The doctor told me to think again, but I had answered that it didn't matter. That's why the baby couldn't come back home and cry. I wept for the first time that day. For my baby.

That lonely night I cried instead of the baby. It was dead, but no one knew and no one had cried. So I cried for everyone else. I couldn't even cry anymore afterwards. But no one will know how hard I tried to look like the old me when I went to work. Even if the man I loved wasn't there, it didn't matter, I still wanted to look like that. But I guess he didn't care about all this. So I thought: I must kill him. I still didn't know what his secret was, but I reckoned I had to kill him for the baby's sake. That's something necessary for any parent with a child who cries alone in the afterlife.

I had everything planned, what I was going to do. I would ask to meet again, and he would take me to an inn, so I put a knife in my bag to kill him. In the bag he had given me as a gift.

I had dinner with him. Do you know what was funny? My heart kept pounding as we were sitting there together. And I remembered how much I had loved this man. That doesn't mean my decision had changed. I thought, I'll kill this guy and we'll die together. Then the three of us could live together in the other world. Because I wasn't sure I could defeat that other woman in this world anyway. I said what I had planned. Do you remember what you told me before? That men are all the same, that's all they ever think about. But he turned me down. He said he had someone he loved. I said it didn't matter. It was love and it was bullshit, and killing him was all I could think of. If he wasn't going to go to bed with me, I could kill him there and then. It didn't matter where. That's when he said it and I finally realised. The secret that he was hiding. It was in my past. The times I've been hiding from him, the ones I want to erase.

I had forgotten. And I was just blaming him for abandoning me. How much did he know about my past? How hurt he must have been when he found out. Like a fool, I was thinking I was the only victim. He was so sweet that he couldn't even tell me that and suffered alone. I realised who the bad guy really was. It was me. I had been imposing my guilt on everyone.

Mum, what would you have done? At least you wouldn't have given up the baby like me. Looking back, I regret all that time. Why did I live so thoughtlessly? Maybe I could start all over again? It might not be too late, as people often say. But, then, what about our baby, who didn't even have a name?

I don't think I can go on living like this. I'll never be a good mother like you. But I still want to be a mother. Mum, you can understand. I'm sorry.

Please understand. I'm just sorry, grateful and sorry. Mum, I love you.

The Symbol

Assassins exist in many other societies and cultures. India, too, had a notorious group. They appeared around the time that the Alamut Assassins fell to the Mongols. It is certainly interesting that one such group disappeared from history just as another emerged.

Unlike in the Ismaili tradition, what distinguished the assassins in India, with its large territories, diverse races, complex cultures and multiple castes, was that they were more closely related to money. They also promoted their religion; however, while religion was the main motive behind the creation of the Alamut Assassins, there was a sort of loose camaraderie that held together the Indian Thuggees. The goddess worshipped by the Indian assassins was Kali. Kali, the goddess of destruction, oversees death. The Indian assassins believed that killing their victims was pleasing to Kali and that they were protected by her. They claimed to be fulfilling their mission according to Kali's myth, but their worship of Kali was more of an excuse than true worship.

Kali is the wife of Shiva, the god of destruction; one of Shiva's many wives, or a different figure of the same wives, or even a feminine figure with Shiva's destructive side. Of course, that is not a strange idea once you understand the religious views of Hindus who believe that there are many gods and that they are all one.

Kali, the goddess of destruction, appears as the most terrible of all the gods in India. With tangled hair, her enemies' heads hang around her neck and her skirts consist of the bodies of her victims. In addition, her tongue is red with the blood of the victim she has just eaten, and she always sticks out her tongue with pride. Each of her hands carries weapons for various forms of killing, with one holding a spear aloft that pierces the devil, while she tramples on her husband, Shiva, with one foot. Like her name, she's a pretty exciting goddess.

The legend of Kali, which the Thuggees used to justify their purpose, was a myth about her fight against the devil Raktabija. Raktabija was the same devil pierced by the spear held by Kali, as described earlier. Raktabija was an unkillable demon because whenever a drop of his blood fell on the earth, a thousand more Raktabijas were born there. So Kali tore off her clothes and gave them to two humans, commanding them to strangle the blood-born Raktabijas. Then she raised Raktabija's body in the air, pierced it with her spear and drank all the blood that flowed down the weapon. An Amazon, indeed! The Thuggees claimed that they were strangling descendants of Raktabija. People who had no money couldn't be descendants of Raktabija, for of course, the descendants of the devil cannot be poor!

Their way of working was neither organised nor professional, unlike the Ismaili Assassins. Their victims were mainly pilgrims and merchants travelling across the vast continent. Disguised as a group of pilgrims themselves, they would fall in with their victim along the road as if by chance. When the traveller had let down his guard sufficiently and they had reached a remote enough place, the assassins would begin their work. While one of the assassins distracted the victim, another would strangle him with a scarf or a rumal, a yellow cloth symbolising the hem of Kali's clothes. Then finally another would dig a hole in the ground and bury the body.

Compared to the Ismaili Assassins, there were certain aspects of the killings that stood out. One was the effectively divided assassination process and the other the attitude that valued secrecy. They assassinated based on reality and profit, at least to some extent, and if they were caught or killed during an assassination, there was no Paradise waiting for them. Once the victim was dead, they took what was in his pockets, buried the body in a remote area and returned home. Just as the caste system was an absolute in Indian society, being part of an assassination squad was also hereditary. But this hereditary succession was simply a secret: only those in the family knew that they were assassins. Their secret could be kept for a long time because they used a special jargon known as Ramasee among themselves. They also had close relationships with the local land owners and the royal family, offering some of their income as taxes or performing other tasks that were not too demanding. Thus, protected by those in power, they could continue as self-sustaining organisations for a long time. Because it was a local and family organisation, it did not have the systematic and uniform power that those in Alamut boasted. They had no political influence and no fortress of their own. Only the yellow rumal, symbolising Kali, that they used to strangle their victims, was an implicit signal that allowed them to recognise and protect each other. Therefore, India's assassination squads never enjoyed the near-mythological notoriety or power enjoyed by the Ismaili Assassins.

However, this fact also allowed them to continue their career quietly for hundreds of years, unlike the Ismaili Assassins, who were wiped out relatively early on. Rumours circulated that assassination squads existed, like some kind of scare story, but no one knew what they were. It's just that a lot of people who left on journeys failed to return every year. I don't know if it's a reliable statistic, but it was claimed that as many as 30,000 people used to go missing each year. Unlike the Ismailis' sporadic operations, the Indian Thuggees were obviously quite busy.

It was thanks to the powerful foreigners who ruled the region that these Indian assassination squads finally disappeared. In the nineteenth century, Britain decided to wipe out the organised crime that was hampering India's development and began a massive clean-up campaign against the assassins. The British were not usually the target of assassins, so they had shown little interest until then. They had regarded the phenomenon as just an exaggerated Indian scare story or a sort of legend. But one day all previous decisions were overturned, and suddenly the British soldiers began to stamp out the assassination squads.

There are two theories. One is that assassination squads had killed British people. After all, the British had long monopolised India's wealth, so it was inevitable that they would be targeted. This theory claims that Britain started to investigate the disappearance of British people in India and launched the clean-up because they discovered that assassination squads were behind it.

Another account is told about a temple of Kali. British troops stationed at the temple reported witnessing an incredible sight: bodies filling the altars, many of which showed signs of having been eaten. Shocked by the horrendous sight, the British interrogated the people in the temple. They told an unbelievable story about the goddess Kali coming down at dawn to eat them. The British troops duly waited until dawn and when Kali didn't come, they determined that the culprits behind this barbaric act must have been the people in the temple, so they killed them. It was said that the bodies in the temple were later discovered to have been killed by the assassins.

Either way, Britain decided to wipe out the assassination squads. Stevenson, a British man who consistently insisted on the need to abolish them, was given the heavy responsibility. Rumoured burial sites were dug up, and hundreds of bodies came pouring out of forests and caves. Extensive arrests, torture and executions were carried out in various parts of the country, and the assassins, who had been notorious for hundreds of years, disappeared.

Nor did their trusted Kali protect them from this fate. The assassins thought they had been abandoned by the goddess, so that their secret was no longer a secret. Most of the arrested Thuggees eventually grew old in prison and no one took over their hereditary profession. But no one knows if all the gang members that Britain got rid of were really assassins. At that time, there were so many Indians who the British decided to arrest and execute as assassins, and torture always produced more names than necessary.

What is at least clear is that today there are no more simple assassination squads that worship the goddess Kali and strangle with a rumal. Travellers moving about on foot or horseback have almost entirely disappeared, and modern means of transportation rarely stop in remote places where it is easy to bury bodies in secret. In fact, it could have been the development of mass transportation that contributed most to the disappearance of India's assassins. The world has become a place where three people can no longer operate as a covert group and strangle travellers. What finally toppled the assassins were an industrialised society and capitalism. They could not adapt to so-called modern society. There are still many organised crime syndicates in India and some claim to be descendants of the assassination squads. But they are nothing more than gangsters who demand protection money and engage in various business dealings. Thus the great assassination squads have disappeared behind the curtain of history.

* * *

The Manager was there when I came back home. She asked me if I was free two days later, and I said it didn't matter. It really didn't matter. I was too tired to think. The Manager said she wanted to see me at work. I nodded instead of answering. Actually, I wanted to ask the Manager a lot of questions; however, it was unlikely that she would know anything about Hyeon-gyeong. She already knew too much about me. If she didn't know what had happened between us, I didn't want to give her any more information. And actually, if the Company was really responsible, she must have known. Maybe it was just shame that stopped me from asking.

'Get some sleep, you look wretched,' she told me, then left.

It was the first time she had told me that. My face really was looking dreadful, and I was sure the Manager knew something. I looked in the mirror. I saw a face, the faint image of the ordinary-looking face of a man, which anyone would forget the moment they turned away. People often tell someone their face looks like a mess. But what was the standard? I didn't know. It was just the face of a murderer. Maybe my face had always been a mess.

She had told me to sleep, but I didn't think I'd get to sleep. I took out a bottle, put it on the table and read Hyeon-gyeong's suicide note again. There was no evidence that it was a fake. But there was no way I could judge that. I had nothing to compare it with to confirm whether or not it was her handwriting, and all I knew about handwriting analysis was basic, how people make a stroke, how they draw letters, how they draw dots or figures. But it wouldn't be hard to fool a handwriting appraiser of my level. Especially if he was drunk, as I was. The contents of the letter were the same as I remembered from our time together. It was oddly specific in some parts, but in some places too abstract. If the Company had been bugging our conversations, it was a level of writing that could be created with a little imagination. And as far as I knew, the Company monitored a target's every move. I decided to withhold judgement. The decision to withhold may have been based on something, but I hardly remember, now that everything is all broken and scattered like shattered pieces of glass. My feelings were just the same then.

Lying back in bed, I sighed, closed my eyes. And I cried. I cried like a child. There was no reason. I just wanted to cry. Then I got out of bed and burned the suicide note over the gas stove. It was an act that I couldn't understand if I thought about it coldly. The suicide note was the only evidence that could reveal the truth about Hyeon-gyeong's death. Maybe it was because I was too drunk. Really.

* * *

It was past noon when I opened my eyes the next day. Yerin was sitting beside my bed.

'I made some rice gruel.'

I got up. Every time I moved, I felt as if someone was stamping on my brain.

'How did you get here?'

My head throbbed every time I spoke.

'Don't you remember?'

I sat down at the table and closed my eyes. I vaguely remembered crying with my head in Yerin's lap. I could feel the tips of my ears turning red.

'Did I phone . . .?'

'Yes. At dawn.'

She went to the gas stove and brought over a pot of rice gruel. She began to skim carefully from the top, where it had cooled.

'Sorry. I made a lot of mistakes yesterday.'

'That's okay,' she said. She put the bowl down in front of me and laid her hand on mine. 'I'm glad you called.'

Her warmth was conveyed through the back of my hand. I was embarrassed because it was an unexpected response.

'When you're done, you have to tell me what happened.'

Yerin stayed with me until that evening. Even though she must have been tired, she didn't show it at all. I sat blankly on the sofa, looking at her and thinking of Hyeon-gyeong. And as I thought about Hyeon-gyeong, I looked at Yerin again. Okay, let's face it. I had killed about thirty people, perhaps one more, maybe two more. If there was a Hell, sin could go to Hell. I felt sorry toward both of them but I didn't want to make Yerin unhappy. Maybe Yerin could accept my past, and I was afraid of that. But there was, for example, a kind of certainty. She was fully capable of understanding. At least, that was the woman I had come to know during our time together. She was such a fabulous woman that I couldn't believe she really existed. I felt she knew everything, and I felt she could accept anything. Wasn't that how she was portrayed even in Hyeon-gyeong's suicide note? Not just me, but anyone else would feel that way about her.

That didn't solve my professional problem. Even if what happened to Hyeon-gyeong could be explained as the result of some unfortunate misunderstandings and inevitable events, I would have to continue to kill people and plan truly successful murders. The high salary I was earning was due to those deaths. So if I quit my job, the money would disappear. And I couldn't be sure that the Company would allow me to quit. If I quit my job and went broke, would she accept me? Or might she be able to accept my killing people? I couldn't imagine either situation. If I really intended to propose, should I hide the fact of my job for the rest of my life or should I be honest and tell her? I only now started thinking foolishly about things I should have thought about before I bought the ring.

That night, alone in my workshop, I made a balance sheet and did a risk analysis as if I was planning a murder. There was no solution. Rather, it was easier to do risk analysis for a murder. I was a little ashamed that it was more difficult to deal with my marriage and the need to reveal the truth than to kill someone. Other people's lives were like that to me after all.

The next day I had an appointment with someone from the Company. I stopped by at Hyeon-gyeong's funeral wake in a black suit early in the morning. None of her bereaved family members recognised me. The people from the office had come yesterday, so I was lost among the other mourners. I wanted to see her face in person, not a portrait, but I couldn't do anything about that. I left the funeral parlour and went round to the back of the building. There I cried a bit, leaning against the outer wall of the building where she seemed to be. It was so confusing. I couldn't understand at all what I felt about her. There was grief, sorrow, guilt, but there was more, too. I knew full well that it was more important than I had imagined, but I had survived and now I was getting married. No one can have everything. Sometimes you have to throw something away to survive. Even if you suspect it's precious.

I poured cement over my complicated feelings and smoothed it off neatly, just like the Mafia disposing of a body. Now I only had to throw the drum into the sea of the unconscious known as oblivion and it would all be over.

The man from the Company was older than I expected. He had a big smile on his face that reminded me of the elderly actor Choi Bool-am.

'You must have been to the funeral.'

He looked at my black suit as he spoke. Instead of answering, I nodded and sat down opposite him.

'What did you want to see me about?'

'Don't rush. We won't have to see each other again if there's nothing special. Let's talk slowly. There must be a lot of things you want to say and hear.'

He said this with an expression suggesting that he knew everything. Somehow, he looked abominable, making me clench my fists.

'No, I know too much already. I'm sick and tired of it.'

He nodded.

'That humble attitude of yours is highly appreciated by the Company.'

How would I be evaluated if I punched his face at that moment?

'First of all, congratulations. You've passed another test.'

'You mean … there's been another test?'

I almost brought up the question of Hyeon-gyeong. But it was no use asking. No matter how he answered, I was sure I wouldn't believe him. Now I could vaguely see what the Company's game was. The Company wasn't making up lies. It was mixing lies with the truth. Then making it all uniform so that the truth didn't exist anywhere. Ask him about Hyeon-gyeong and he'd say something. And if you asked him about her again, he'd answer, 'Well, in a way.' Just like that. For them, everything was only a matter of perspective. Hyeon-gyeong could have committed suicide, or faked a suicide, it could be because of me, or it could be manipulation. In the process, Hyeon-gyeong may have been pregnant with my child and had an abortion, or that may also be another lie. The bottom line was that I could never believe their answers. Of course, by burning her suicide note while I was drunk, I'd come to agree with their plan.

He leaned against the backrest. And said, with a humorous expression, 'Even we don't know if there are other tests.'

I barely managed to hold back the curse that was on the tip of my tongue. It was not wise to be angry. I needed to elicit more information by engaging in a dialogue that was as friendly as possible. Only the Company knew the truth about what had happened to me. I reflected on his answer carefully. It was possible he didn't know. But he used the term 'we'. In other words, not only he, but even the Company did not know. Maybe he was one of the key people in the Company. So it could be that they made joint decisions on any matter that the Company decided.

'You mean that the Company has no say in the tests?'

'You're mistaken. Testing is not done by the Company,' he replied with a polite smile.

My throat ached.

'What?'

'The Company doesn't need anyone. Not only can it withstand any threat, but it is also doubtful that there is any threat to the Company.'

I had no idea what the hell he was talking about. He was observing my reactions carefully and enjoying them. I couldn't do anything about it. The one who always has more secrets holds the key.

'If the Company tests someone, it's not to keep secrets or ward off threats. It's to see who's qualified. And to some extent for your safety. You're important. As long as the Company needs you.'

Ultimately, it was no different from talk about a driver's licence. It was not a question of eligibility, it was not about 007's licence to kill.

'The way we test is simple. When there is enough of a threat to someone, it's just a matter of putting a little stone in the way. We have no other motivation. It's important for us to know who someone is, basically. If they're important, we have to protect them.'

Was the little stone Hyeon-gyeong's suicide note, or was it making a murder plan for her, or was it all of it? He was saying that the Company had set a test to protect me. It didn't make any sense.

'So if you collapse, there's nothing we can do about it, and if you don't collapse, we'll tell you a little bit more. Of the truth.'

The corners of his mouth went up slightly.

'After all, the truth hurts.'

Mazes of words. He was fooling around with me. All right, I was willing to take it. If it meant I could know the truth.

'So what's the truth?'

He bowed his head. At that moment, I realised he was holding back his laughter. I thought: *How long will it take to kill him if I strangle him?*

'I don't understand why you're asking. I reckon you already know the answer.'

Suddenly, I felt my body slowly sinking into the chair I was sitting on. The cement-filled drum containing Hyeon-gyeong was rising again from the abyss. I could see why the Company had tried to kill her, according to him at least. It was because she was trying to kill me. But was that true? He was smiling. I wanted to cut his throat, pull his guts out and scatter them, but I couldn't move. Slowly, my neck was growing stiff.

'Of course, I don't think you're acknowledging it yet.'

He took out his handkerchief and covered his mouth with it, taking short, fitful breaths. His face, as he held back his laughter, filled my vision. He tilted his upper body closer to me. I longed to rip out his tongue right there, but anything I did would only delight him more. The man was enjoying my pain, my suffering. The more I suffered, the better. I closed my eyes and took a deep breath. Hyeon-gyeong's arm was just coming out of the drum.

He whispered, 'That's a lot of self-control. I thought I'd get hit. You're a better person for the Company than I expected. I'll give you something good as a prize.'

He pulled out a notepad, still keeping his upper body in the same position, drew something on a blank page and handed it to me. There was a picture on the memo. It showed two triangles, one either side of a diamond shape, forming a large triangle overall. I couldn't put my finger on it, but I thought I'd seen it somewhere before.

'It's the Company's symbol. Of course, we don't use it officially. Even if we use it, we make a lot of changes within this basic form.'

It was a little surprising that there was a symbol for the Company. It did not match the image of it that I had envisioned so far.

'You look surprised. But you should realise that the Company is a broad and loose organisation. Sometimes we have to cooperate without knowing each other's identity, and we need this symbol.'

'What does it stand for?'

'The principle of order by which this world exists. The big triangle symbolises power. The food chain of the ecosystem, the powerful dominance of the pyramid and the stability of the triangle. It's the most stable shape. And the diamond-shaped trapezoid in it symbolises our society. You learned about that at school, too. This is the class structure of modern society. A few people in the upper class, a few in the lower classes, and a wide middle class. It's interesting, isn't it, that there really is such a society?'

I pointed my finger at the triangles either side of the diamond.

'What does this mean?'

'It's something a diamond needs to stand on. Diamonds can never stand on their own. That's why they need triangles of some kind to support them. Making the world as a whole, a big triangle again … It's varied. It's very varied. There are so many beings in the world.'

He was talking nonsense. He looked at me with a proud expression as if the Company was responsible for every kind of order in the world. Why had the Company sent this crazy megalomaniac? Claiming to be telling me the truth? He was only playing with words. He went on:

'You don't know much about it right now. But you'll find out soon. Sooner or later. Having seen you, I think it'll be sooner than I thought. Let me give you a hint: everyone we have killed is also part of this small triangle.'

He leaned back again. For a moment we drank our tea quietly. My mind was buzzing. Hyeon-gyeong had crawled out of the drum now and wrapped her arms around my neck. Everything I had wanted to hide had come fully back to life. I thought of the things he had talked about. There was a hidden intention that I didn't know. Whatever it was, he got up from his seat.

'We'll be getting advice on a variety of things in the Company. And your pay will increase significantly. First of all, you've passed the test, so to speak, and been promoted. Don't be too hostile to the Company. They're a funny lot, so I'm telling you personally. Well, you'll find out soon enough. The tests never end. They never really start.'

He reached out and picked up the note with the picture he had drawn.

'You'll know when you realise the meaning of this drawing. Eventually ... You'll either accept it all or resign yourself to it.'

He smiled gently. Then he crumpled up the page in his hand and left.

I was left behind. I thought about the painful truth I had tried to deny and the mystery he had thrown at me. Yes, I couldn't help but admit it. I was being cowardly about Hyeon-gyeong's death. Whether she was killed by the Company or had killed herself, ultimately it was my responsibility. The child. ... had probably really been there. Even if it was a suicide note constructed by the Company, they had no reason to write it with those contents. That's probably why I had no choice but to burn it. What else could I do? I'd already stabbed her in the heart countless times and strangled her, too. I would do anything to save her and save the child she bore. But such a thing was impossible. There was nothing I could do about it now.

Maybe I'd never see the man again. But it was clear that what he told me would soon turn into something else. Otherwise there was no reason for the Company to have sent him to me.

It didn't take long for me to realise why he explained the Company's symbol so kindly to me. And I was bewitched. But what I needed to listen to more carefully was the last thing he said, that I would either accept or resign myself to everything in the end. Accept or resign … What was the distance between these two words?

Bewitched

I came back home. I searched every corner, but there was nothing left to drink. I lay in bed smoking because I didn't have the energy to go out and buy more liquor. It wasn't like me. But I wanted to do something that wasn't like me. The cigarette smoke, which spread over the black ceiling, constantly melted into the darkness, creating mysterious figures. I tried to imagine something recognisable, but I couldn't imagine anything until the cigarette had burned down. It was just cigarette smoke.

I took out the ring I'd bought for Yerin. The diamond was beautiful. The small, transparent, hard lump of carbon glistened brilliantly in the light of the desk lamp. Suddenly I remembered what the man had said. I looked at the stands supporting the diamond. They were curved triangles. The most stable form. Small triangles. His words were still incomprehensible. Anyway, I had to cheer up and propose. That was the most important thing to me right now. I knew how ugly I was. But I'd already come all the way here, leaving a lot of people's blood behind. The living must live, leaving all that shame, guilt and humiliation behind.

I went into the kitchen to refresh myself, and made simple fried rice by scraping together the side dishes that remained in the refrigerator. I sat in the living room alone with the TV on and ate fried rice while watching a movie. There was a Japanese horror movie from the sixties playing. The actors were exaggerating in a terribly theatrical set, like a really old movie. The blood looked like paint and the ghost was covered with white powder. The movie, a series of short stories, was quite boring, but I didn't have the energy to change channels. At the end of one short story began another of Yuki-onna, the Snow Woman.

The story goes like this. On an unusually cold, snowy night, a boy is returning to his village with an old man after gathering firewood. The snow and the storm prevent the ferry boat from crossing so they fall asleep in a grassy hut next to the ferry. Late at night, the boy wakes up in the biting cold and realises that Yuki-onna is stealing the breath of the old man sleeping next to him. The old man soon freezes to death, then Yuki-onna turns her head and makes eye contact with the boy. When she says he must die because he has seen her, the boy begs her to save his old mother, saying that if he dies, his old mother will be left alone. The snow woman, grown weak-hearted, makes a suggestion. She says that she will let him live if he doesn't tell anyone that he saw her. The boy vows to keep his promise, and she says she will show up and kill the boy if ever he breaks his promise. The next day the storm stops and the boy returns home, telling no one the real reason why the old man died.

The following spring, the boy's mother meets a beautiful girl beside the ferry. The girl says she has left her home to reduce the number of mouths to feed and is on her way to work as a maid for a wealthy family in Tokyo. The boy's mother invites her to spend the night at her house as the sun is setting. The girl goes to the boy's house and the two are drawn to each other. The boy's mother slyly suggests that rather than going to Tokyo to suffer, she should marry her son.

Time passes and the boy becomes a young man. His wife is now quite a mature woman with a reputation as a faithful wife who does everything around the village, and they have children, too. The boy's mother, satisfied to see the two living happily, closes her eyes peacefully. The boy is now a middle-aged man. The children have grown a lot, but the boy's wife is still young and beautiful.

Late one winter's night, the husband, who is weaving straw shoes and talking beside the sleeping children, suddenly sees the snowstorm outside and recalls Yuki-onna. So he tells his wife about the snow woman he saw when he was young. The expression on his wife's face slowly changes as she hears the story. The husband, who had been talking for a long time, suddenly realises that the face of the snow woman he saw at that time is the same as that of his wife.

At that point I changed channels because I suddenly realised that it was the same story as the episode about Gumiho in *Korean Ghost Stories* that I watched when I was young. But I was curious. Which side had copied it from the other? In fact, it was not difficult to infer the answer. Ever since 'Bunsinsama', which was based on 'Gokurisang', I knew that many scary stories were not originally from Korea. I did not know whether it was the influence of the Japanese colonial period, a mere copy of things Japanese, or where the original story had come from. As expected, there were only documentaries to watch on the other channels.

While channel-switching, I found a documentary about what would happen on Earth if humans disappeared. On the screen, a nuclear power plant that had lost its cooling water was melting beyond the critical point. I went back to my bedroom and fell asleep with the TV on. Thanks to the faint sound of advertisements penetrating my dreams, dreams and advertisements got mixed. My beloved Yerin was advertising chocolate and mobile phones, while endless snow fell on them. Then those things changed back into the car in my memory. In the distance, the nuclear power plant that had crossed the critical point exploded, and the snow turned into fallout, making everything white.

When I woke up in the morning, my head was clear and all my thoughts were precise. Sorrowful feelings, complex thoughts, faint suspicions and heavy emotions had all disappeared like dreams. The wisest way to survive is to surrender to the inevitable quickly. I called her. I said let's meet tonight, and she said I should come to her house. I was going to propose. I wanted to rent a place so grandiose and colourful that we would never forget it. But if I prepared such a thing, I felt like I would be subject to chaos again. There was no time because I knew that even the slightest thing could bring back memories of Hyeon-gyeong. So I said I'd go to her house.

After taking the ring from the drawer, I searched the closet. I didn't have anything to wear. I had my hair cut at a hair salon and went to buy clothes before the appointed time. As I roamed the stores with their famous brands, a date with Hyeon-gyeong came to mind. And suddenly, I realised that all the exchanges of emotion I had experienced with Hyeon-gyeong had been replaced by brands. It wasn't a very good memory to recall just before a proposal. It was beyond belief. I could easily forget most anything. I planned to kill someone and the moment I turned around,

I forgot. At times it didn't bother me to look at obituary articles about a person who had been the subject of a plan. I didn't even recognise them, but then, after a while, I'd think, 'Ah, of course,' evoking dry memories without emotion. So why didn't her memory fade away like a shadow?

On my way to Yerin's house, I bought a bouquet of flowers and some champagne. It was my first time going there anyway. I had walked in and out countless times when seeing her home, but always only to the front door. Suddenly, I wondered whether I was not in too much of a hurry to enter her house for the first time. But it didn't matter, because although I wasn't sure how she felt, my heart was clear. And that was the only thing I could be sure of in my life now. If life is shaking precariously at some point, you can just start with what is possible. That was exactly what this proposal was about. I knew I was a coward. But what else could I do? All of this was not a life I had chosen. At some point, the Company gave me a push in the back and I came all this way. And now, I had the right to choose happiness.

When I arrived in front of her house, I saw her outside, in the car park of the apartment. There was nothing to fear. Because in that place there was a guaranteed happiness for me.

Her home resembled her. She expressed the warmth of her inner self by hanging her illustrations in a simple, modern interior. It was like a house in some interior design book or TV advertisement featuring a sophisticated single woman. It was the opposite of my place, which was a small chaos even though it was spacious and had few items of furniture. Suddenly, I was ashamed of the time I had spent with her at my house. I could feel my pulse accelerating as I looked around her house. The fateful moment was approaching. However, at the same time, I could feel something casting a shadow in one corner of my mind. It was like a real shadow. The more she shone, the more uncontrollably I felt for her, and the deeper it became. Maybe it was my conscience. Was this right after all I did to make Hyeon-gyeong so unhappy? But I concluded that it must be a fear of rejection. I was a coward, as every cowardly decision I had made had proved so well. So now it was time for me to admit my fear and propose like an adult.

I ate the meal that she had prepared. She made a pretty good salad and a very good steak. Every time I put food in my mouth and savoured it, I could sense the happiness of decades to come slowly approaching on the tip of my tongue. She also clearly seemed to have a hunch that something special was going to happen, so we encouraged each other. It was a moment when I needed just a tiny scrap more courage.

I finished eating and we went to her bedroom. She asked me to wait a minute while she prepared tea. I stayed there alone, looking around the room. It was neat, like her. A vase was filled with the flowers I had bought, and everything was in order except for a few art books on her desk and paint marks on the workstation. Right next to the door was an illustration she had drawn. It showed characters I had seen in a magazine advertisement, dynamically moving forward. I was a little surprised to realise that she was a more famous illustrator than I had thought, because she was still young. It was clear that her success must be an extremely exceptional case in her company, perhaps not befitting her age. So I was a little more intimidated.

In the illustration, the three central figures were posed in a running position as if they were about to pop out of the screen. It was a rather typical composition in which two sub-characters in each corner were looking up in opposite directions. However, the unique vitality was alive. Maybe because it was an ad.

While I was looking at the picture, she brought in tea and fruit. I took the tray she was carrying and put it down on the small table beside the bed and led her next to it with an arm wrapped around her shoulders. I was going to put her in front of me, kneel down and hold out my ring. I thought it was such a clichéd and childish way to do it, but I was sure it would work, typical composition and traditional methods always having a high probability of success. Once she was in position I put my hand in my pocket and looked at her as she stood with a puzzled expression on her face while I tried to take out the ring. Just at that moment, behind her lovely face, an illustration caught my eye. Her face was hiding the characters, so I could only see the overall composition of the picture.

Suddenly, I realised the identity of the shadow that had been hovering around me. The composition of the picture was exactly the same as the symbol that the person from the Company had showed me. A diamond shape of three characters running out and triangles made by two sub-characters. As I said earlier, it was a typical, common composition. *There's no problem.* Then I remembered the movie that I'd watched the previous day. Was it because the memory of her was so deeply intertwined with snow? What shape was her CD rack in the living room? It was also shaped like four small triangles forming one large one. In other words, it could be seen as a diamond-shaped figure with two triangles. I knew it couldn't be any kind of proof that she had anything to do with the Company. There were countless such CD racks. But I remembered what the man had said. The tests never end. Was Yerin planted by the Company? In that case, what would happen when I confessed to her about the Company? All these thoughts took a very short time, less than two seconds, to come rising up. Numerous thoughts were screaming in unison as if they were about to burst out. I literally froze. When she saw my expression, she asked, 'What's wrong? That look on your face …'

I tried to smile. Then I took the hand that had been clutching the ring out of my pocket and put it back round her shoulders.

Turning her toward the illustration, I said: 'Did you draw this? Wow! You're a far greater artist than I realised.'

It was a clumsy performance. But I want to applaud myself for my response at that moment. It was no different from using a finger to plug a hole in a collapsing dyke. Nevertheless, I did not want to give up hope. All of this was clearly due to my excessive nervousness. Surely I was being ridiculous? From the Company saying how amazing I was, to this. Suddenly, the Manager's face came into my mind. The goddess of my wet dreams. Then I started to wonder about the limits of what the Company could do to me. 'Propose. It's just for the stupid reason you're afraid you'll be rejected,' I kept muttering to myself. But my body refused to move. Yerin asked me if I was okay, and I replied in a trembling voice that I had some kind of indigestion.

I sat in the bathroom and thought, *Stop this stupid delusion and propose.* When I looked up, I noticed the pattern of the tiles beside the bathtub. Unusually, the tiles in her bathroom were triangular, resembling the company's symbol. At that moment, I realised that the man sent from the Company had bewitched me. I couldn't move.

That day, I wasn't able to propose to Yerin. Once again, I could feel that my life, or the life I had dreamed of, was being utterly shattered. The last support, which I had tried to use as a foothold, had been pulled out. I had nothing left now.

I have a million things to say about the symbol he showed me. There is a game called *The Legend of Zelda*. The symbol of the Tri Force in that game is in the shape of a triangle divided into triangles. Some of the nation's leading conglomerates used the same form before changing to initials. In addition, if you search the internet, there are still countless companies that use similar symbols. Universities, research institutes, sports teams, there are enough triangles to make you feel sick of them. According to a book on design, the triangle is one of the forms most favoured by businesses. The reason is that it symbolises stability. Not only that. I've seen exactly the same form of cabinet in the cosmetics section of a department store. There is also the same form of CD rack as Yerin has, and the same form of bookshelf. The glass pyramid of the Louvre Museum in Paris, France, also looks like that. Such patterns are so numerous that they can be found even among the fretwork of old Korean door frames. Should I feel scared and freeze every time? Or should I pay tribute to the influence and power of the Company?

It was ridiculous. My tiny scrap of courage and my glass-like nerves were cursed. Even the eye in the pyramid on the American dollar was a variation of the Company's symbol. I was obviously having a nervous breakdown. But at every moment, everything the Manager had said about Hyeongyeong, the man's words and Yerin's incredible attitude intertwined, turning into something completely different.

I remembered how she had said: 'Though flowers bloom easily, to be beautiful is not easy.' It was a very catchy expression.

It was a very catchy expression. How was I supposed to take it? There was a way to check. I could ask the person who knew me and the Company best.

Questions

Until just before the Manager appeared in front of me that day, I kept running over in my mind the questions I was going to ask her. There must never be a gap. I tried to analyse the risks by considering every imaginable possibility and any number of cases that might emerge. There were too many variables. Things like analysis meant nothing. That was true, yet I couldn't just consult myself. I kept muttering: 'I can't figure out anything in this stupid way.' But I couldn't stop. How could I stop? The last foothold was falling apart. If I was ever to rebuild the collapsed scaffolding, I had to grab on to something, even if it was only dried up, twisted grass roots. But what I was really afraid of was what would be waiting for me afterwards. Could I handle the truth of all this? I suddenly realised that these were the questions I had asked myself when I first decided to accept this job. How much had I really changed since then?

I met the Manager in a bar in the basement of a hotel. It was the first time we had gone drinking together. I felt confident that she would not refuse. She was my Manager, and it was clear that she would know what had happened to me, at least as much as she needed to know. After all, she had even told me to eat well.

The Manager arrived on time, which was like her, but now I had to destroy that image of her. If I didn't get through that shell, I would never hear the truth. We simply exchanged greetings and ordered cocktails. She ordered a Bloody Mary and I ordered a Martini. Both of us emptied three glasses without saying much. It felt as if we were looking at each other with guns aimed. Perhaps from my silence she could guess what I was going to say. Even so, she had better get drunk. The bartender who was cleaning the table took the hint and went to the other side of the bar. The first blow was important.

I whispered in her ear, 'I want to fuck you.'

The Manager laughed. She leaned against the bar and laughed loudly as if she had heard a great joke. Everyone in the bar looked at us. Embarrassed, I slowly emptied my glass, with the look on my face of a child caught playing a practical joke.

'What do you want to know?'

As expected, she was competent. I had wanted her to be more embarrassed, but I couldn't help it.

'If I tell you, will you answer?'

'Will you believe my answer?'

I kept aimlessly chewing olives, and put my hand on hers as it lay on the bar. She giggled.

'Saying that physical contact is forbidden is a lie, isn't it?' I whispered to her in the most lovey-dovey way I could imagine.

'Don't act so poorly. It's funny.' She quickly pulled away her pale hand and picked up her handbag. There seemed to be no way. At that moment, a thought crossed my mind.

'What happens to you if something unfortunate happens to me?'

Her hands stopped moving for a moment. She put down her bag.

'What are you talking about?'

'For example, what happens if I get into an accident, die of an overdose of sleeping pills or get ruined by alcoholism, that kind of thing.'

She looked shaken. It was obvious that it had worked. I swallowed.

'That's ridiculous.'

'Don't be so sure. The guy from the Company I met the day before yesterday said so. It's not for the Company, it's for me. Nothing can threaten the Company. But what happens to the Company if they lose me?'

'They'll find someone else. There's plenty of other people.'

She spoke lightly. But I didn't miss a subtle change of expression.

'Then are you going to rip off your face again?'

There was a moment of silence. Then I heard her sigh.

'I can't tell you what I know, because the Company has decided it's better for you.'

'I guessed so. I think so, too. I'm just grateful to the Company. But now I want to decide something for myself.'

She tapped the bar nervously with the tips of her nails. Then the tapping stopped at some point.

'Okay, just one thing.'

'Does Yerin belong to the Company?'

Suddenly she looked pathetic and leaned forward with the tip of her thumbnail hooked over the edge of the bar. The false nail attached to it fell off.

'Why are you asking me that?'

She did the same thing with another finger. Another nail fell off.

'Ask her yourself some time.'

Again, another nail fell off.

'Why do you want to fuck me?'

Yet another nail fell off.

'Why was Hyeon-gyeong not acceptable to you?'

And the false nail on her pinkie dropped off.

'Was she not your perfect, ideal type?'

All her false nails having fallen off, she raised her hand to show the bare nails.

'You're asking me about things that you don't need to ask me. You just don't want to make your own decisions.'

It was a sharp insight. It was so sharp that every word she spoke was like a blade piercing my heart. I had nothing to say. I lowered my head. On the bar lay the nails that had fallen from her fingers, colourfully painted. Quite beautiful. I got up. She said she would pay. I left the hotel.

There were taxis lined up in front of the hotel, but I walked away, ignoring them. My attempt to consult the Manager about my life had failed. I looked at the lights shining in each house along the Namsan Ring Road and recalled the questions she'd asked me. It was time for me to decide for myself.

Why did I want to fuck her? The Company had made her for me, or rather for the Company. Why hadn't they been able to accept Hyeon-gyeong? She was a woman whose extremely real flaws were conspicuous. That couldn't have been the problem. It's something that everyone has.

Why was Yerin my ideal type? She had the same tastes as me, I liked the way she looked, and she did things that I thought were ideal. Like the luxury goods that Hyeon-gyeong loved.

The man from the Company said the tests were for me. When I fell in love and proposed to someone and revealed my job, I would be the one who would suffer the most if the consequences were tragic. And that might have an impact on my work. Maybe that was the last thing the Company wanted. It was too perfect a fit. But there was a problem with one premise. Was Hyeon-gyeong's suicide note really written by her? It was cowardly of me to ask this question again. But I couldn't be sure of anything, even something so small. He had also said that the tests never end. Then maybe that too was something that the Company planned. If Yerin was from the Company, did she love me or was all this just a delusion? All uncertainty was excluded from my life. But suddenly everything was uncertain. Of course, if it was the Company's plan, even that would be just another trajectory I didn't know. For the first time, I felt a sense of distance from a life lived according to the Company's decisions. If I didn't like it, at that very moment, I had to decide for myself in the midst of all this chaos, but I couldn't answer. I had never made a decision on my own.

Conclusion

I think I'm going to stop writing now. What will the Company think about what I have written? I don't know. If this is made public, maybe I too will experience a natural death. In the end, everyone dies. Maybe you will not believe what I have written. You think the existence of the Company is some kind of metaphor or symbol. But I couldn't help but write down what I've come to know. Like Midas's barber, whispering the king's secret to the reeds, I couldn't bury in my heart what people should know. I am writing this in order to forget the pain of the secrets I have had to know. This is my way of resisting the Company. Although I know it won't hurt the Company a bit, I want you to know. The Company exists and we live in it. There are no exceptions.

Eventually, I married the Manager. The ring that I gave her when I proposed was the same one I originally intended to give to Yerin. I don't know if she's aware of that. Anyway, she was happy. Or at least she looked as if she was. Diamonds are forever.

It was a normal wedding ceremony except for the almost complete lack of friends from the groom's side. The wedding planner deftly replied, 'There are quite a few cases like this nowadays,' and assigned her own boyfriends and office companions to stand on the bridegroom's side for the pictures taken after the ceremony. I also asked some cousins my age to stand in for me. So a pretty plausible wedding photo came out. Like everyone, we got married in an hour and were out of our minds on the wedding day, so the only thing left was the pictures. Even so, I've only ever opened the album a few times during our house-warming party.

The Manager, now my wife, eventually had a saline bag pulled out of her breast. The fibrosis had got so severe that she had to undergo surgery again, but I told her I didn't care if her bosom was small, it was okay, there was already enough hypocrisy in our lives. But I could never make up my mind whether what I said about a small bosom being sufficient was a lie or not. I said I don't care about her breasts, but I still watch porn featuring women with big breasts. I decided not to dwell on that either. Like a lot of other issues. If you don't want to make excuses, pretend you don't know. Just like everyone else.

One of the things I learned when I got married was that, unexpectedly, she attended church. The demon of my wet dreams was also an ordinary, commonplace person. Eventually, her preaching persuaded me to go to church, too. I would never have gone if it weren't for those Christmas memories of original sin.

Isn't it amazing that Heaven belongs to us after all? Apart from those who haven't acknowledged the Lord. But nothing will change for them. I've already seen Hell.

One of the things that surprised me while attending church was that Christianity had a fairly rational, computational mechanism. I finally understood how Christianity and the Greek philosophy that I had memorised in high school gave birth to capitalism. If we live in sin for six days of the week then go on Sunday to acknowledge and confess Jesus as Lord, all our sins disappear. Because our Absolute One is always overflowing with love and forgives all sins. So we can go to Heaven. That wasn't bad. But what happens to the sins that we don't recognise, and those that aren't forgiven? I don't know.

If I could choose the time of my death, I would choose Sunday afternoon. Then Heaven is as good as reserved in advance.

Last week, the pastor preached about the Sermon on the Mount. This sermon, which reminds me of the Old Man of the Mountain, is about the eight blessings Jesus proclaimed on the mountain. The first phrase starts like this.

Blessed are the poor in spirit, for the Kingdom of Heaven is theirs.

I couldn't understand what it meant to be poor in spirit. The pastor went on about longing for God, but it didn't make sense that longing for God meant being poor in spirit. So I looked up the data. That's the second-best thing to do after making excuses and planning to kill someone. The same verse appears in the Gospel of Luke, which was written before Matthew's, where the word 'spirit' is omitted and it only says 'Blessed are the poor'. The reason why Matthew, who came later than Luke, is different is because the believers of Matthew's church, for whom the author wrote the gospel, were mainly rich. The author, who referred to the Gospel of Luke, added the phrase 'in spirit' in order to send his beloved believers to Heaven.

Now the gates of Heaven have opened for the rich. About two thousand years later, it was one of the countless indulgences that would appear thanks to Max Weber, who argued that profit-seeking was never a sin and that compulsions and greed were in accordance with the Christian spirit. Weber thought the accumulation of wealth was in line with the spirit of Protestantism. It's not a crime, so long as it's reasonable. On that foundation, our lives and now the Company have been created. But I don't know what's reasonable.

Anyway, that's how we go to Heaven. I feel like crying with happiness.

Last month, the number of people I have caused to die a natural death passed fifty. Not counting, of course, the fifteen pigs. So much for the people I can count. But what about all the people I may have killed in my life without realising it?

The Manager gave birth to her first child six months after marrying me. A daughter. Life is beautiful. She said she would raise our child to be a good and pretty child. The child is so small and fragile that it seems she will disappear if touched, and the tip of her nose is dazzlingly lovely. Sometimes, when I see the baby, I am reminded of the child that could not be born. Was it a boy or a girl? Holding the small, vulnerable baby in my arms, I tried to imagine how many more people she would cause to die once she grew up. I felt dizzy. I just hope she survives as long as possible and kills fewer people than I or other people. That's probably what it means to be good

Better still, after giving birth to the baby, the Manager has grown a lot gentler and now she talks about the Company much more readily than before. So I finally found out the answer to the riddle of her appearance. When I asked how she created the face that I thought was the sexiest in the Company, she replied with a smile.

'It's simple. When you were stuck in the condo and downloaded Japanese porn every day, the face recognition programme combined the type of actress you prefer, the maximum number of downloads, and their frequency, to produce this face. It's similar to studying people's patterns of consumption of famous brands.'

It's a world where you can even analyse tastes. There was no reason for desire to be an exception. However, it was such a boring method that I was a bit disappointed. I'd been wondering for quite a while. So the Company also worked on the basis of ordinary market research. There was no special, absolute power. Now the Company isn't as frightening as it used to be. I'm much more afraid of myself than of the Company. And most afraid of ordinary people.

Other than that, nothing much has happened in the past three years. Sometimes I look back on the past and think about the choices I've made. But I know my excuses will remain the same, as the Manager once told me. That's who I am. I sometimes remember what I heard from the Company person I met a long time ago, after Hyeon-gyeong died. The man who reminded me of Choi Bool-am. Ultimately, either I should accept it all or resign.

Sometimes, though, there are nights full of nightmares, dreams where I kill everyone I know, even my child, with my own hands, and remain alone. When I wake up after such a dream, it's hard to distinguish reality from dream. I barely feel relieved after confirming that my wife is breathing next to me in bed. After I have woken up properly, for a long time I look at my daughter's face as she lies in her cot. Then I go and cry alone in the living room. My stifled weeping in the dark living room with the lights turned off brings back a lot of thoughts and memories, things I want to believe I've forgotten. Then I get so scared that my whole body trembles. What's really scary is the fact that I've already killed before and it won't be hard to kill again. It doesn't matter either. Is my love for them really love? Should I kill someone else with that love? Maybe they were also part of another plan to tie me to the Company? Then the nightmare becomes a reality, and the world feels like another Hell.

Apart from that, I am happy. In the end, might that be called a happy ending?

Last week, we took the child on a picnic. She has passed her first birthday now. While pushing the stroller in a sunny park, I stopped and looked at my hand. It was a fine hand with no sign of labour. I raised my hand and smelled it. It smelled of soap. There were quite a lot of people like me around. Everyone looked happy. I heard a child laughing somewhere.

It's happiness. Happiness with the smell of blood.

A WORD FROM THE AUTHOR

An unusually high number of people were fired that year. The bankruptcy of Lehman Brothers the year before had caused many companies to go bust or lay off workers. Everywhere I went, there was only talk of restructuring. It was around this time that I received a phone call from a friend who had lost his job at a company he worked for. One day, while passing in front of the intersection where the headquarters of a large corporation was located, I witnessed a union rally. A banner was hung behind the protesters. It said:

'Restructuring is murder.'

There was a reason why this term appeared. At that time, a documentary aired on TV had tracked the results of a company's restructuring and reported on the current lives of former employees. In many cases, workers who had been engaged in the field for a long time had failed to find a new job and suffered from hardship, while not a small number of them took their own lives.

When I saw the words on the banner, I suddenly became curious: there must be a perpetrator for it to be murder, but who was the perpetrator? Was it the employee in charge of restructuring? No. He was just doing his job as an employee. Or was it the representative or executive who directed the restructuring? The biggest reason for this crisis was an external financial crunch, so I thought it would be difficult to hold them accountable. So I went back and thought about it more.

A fund manager at Lehman Brothers? Someone who designed a COD called sub-prime mortgage loan? An investment bank that rode on and fuelled a bubble? Someone who rode on the bubble, sprinkled bonuses around and proposed toasts...?

But it was impossible to pinpoint any one person and hold them accountable. It was someone's fault, but I couldn't name who it really was, and I couldn't ask for a reasonable compensation from anyone. Alas, this is the perfect murder. I couldn't help but marvel. Oh my God! Here's a real thriller!

Not surprisingly, the poorer the country, the higher these waves would be. So, in some of the poorest countries, the whole country was devastated as if by a tsunami. The biggest victims of sub-prime mortgages were the poorest people, who didn't even know what they were. How many people had been swept away by this wave? But does anyone who is responsible for this know about it? Do they feel any remorse? Easy money went to them in the name of bailouts, and probably in all likelihood, they did very well out of it. without any feeling of guilt.

So I couldn't help but write.

And now, ten years later, the novel has been translated into English like this. Even though this book was inspired by events that were worldwide, only Korean readers could read it. However, now, with the help of agents, translators, editors and publishers, I am able to meet English-speaking readers like this. Thank you very much. Thanks again for all the hard work. The fact that it has been translated like this now means that the above questions are still valid, even though time has passed. Right? So what do my new readers think?

A NOTE ON THE AUTHOR
AND THE TRANSLATOR

IM SEONG-SUN majored in Literature back in college, before starting his writing career as assistant director for two films. Realising he couldn't write his own stories with investors in mind, however, he wrote his first novel *The Consultant*, which won the 2010 Segye Literary Award. Since then, he has written ten books, and won Korea's Young Artist Award for his short story 'The Sheeple Wandering a Gallery and their Predators,' and the Korean SF Award for his sci-fi novel *Ouroboros*. He writes scripts and adapts books for commercial films, and is currently working on a TV series.

AN SEON JAE (aka Brother Anthony of Taizé) was born in England in 1942. He studied at the Queen's College in Oxford. He joined the Community of Taizé in 1969. He has been living in Korea since 1980, and taught English literature at Sogang University, where he is now an emeritus professor, until he retired in 2007. He is also a chair-professor at Dankook University. He has translated works by many major contemporary Korean writers, mostly poetry, publishing well over 50 volumes. He served as President of the Royal Asiatic Society (Korea) for ten years and is now its President Emeritus. He was awarded an Honorary MBE in 2015. His home page URL is http://anthony.sogang.ac.kr/

A NOTE ON THE TYPE

The text of this book is set in Minion, a digital typeface designed by Robert Slimbach in 1990 for Adobe Systems. The name comes from the traditional naming system for type sizes, in which minion is between nonpareil and brevier. It is inspired by late Renaissance-era type.